CHILD CARE

for

L O V E

or

MONEY?

CHILD CARE
for
L O V E
or
MONEY?

A Guide to
Navigating the
Parent–Caregiver
Relationship

JOSEPH A. CANCELMO, Psy.D.
CAROL BANDINI, Ph.D.

JASON ARONSON INC.
Northvale, New Jersey
London

Production Editor: Elaine Lindenblatt

This book was set in 11 pt. New Century Schoolbook and printed and bound by Book-mart Press, Inc. of North Bergen, NJ.

Library of Congress Cataloging-in-Publication Data

Cancelmo, Joseph A.
    Child care for love or money : a guide to navigating the parent–caregiver relationship / Joseph A. Cancelmo and Carol Bandini.
        p. cm.
    Includes bibliographical references and index.
    ISBN 0-7657-0178-2
    1. Child care. 2. Caregivers. 3. Child care workers.
    4. Parents. I. Bandini, Carol. II. Title.
    HQ778.5.C36   1998
    649'.1—DC21   98–20599

Printed in the United States of America on acid-free paper. For information and catalog write to Jason Aronson Inc., 230 Livingston Street, Northvale, NJ 07647-1726. Or visit our website: www.aronson.com

To the memory of
Joseph C. Cancelmo, Staceyann Gordon,
and Thomas M. Malloy;
all were more than "good-enough" caregivers
in their own unique ways.

J. A. C.

For Robert, who is with me through it all.

C. B.

Contents

PART II: A GUIDE TO THE
PARENT–CAREGIVER RELATIONSHIP

Acknowledgments

Help came from many directions in writing this book. We thank the men and women—parents and caregivers—who were so willing to be interviewed. They helped reveal the complexities, strengths, and struggles within this relationship. We are indebted to the Summit Child Care Centers of Summit, New Jersey, and to Florence Nelson, Ph.D., Executive Director. The Summit staff graciously gave us their time and wisdom, evidence of many years of rich experience. Joan Friedman, owner of A Choice Nanny in New York City, was generous with her time, insights, and assistance with parent and caregiver interviewing. In particular, we are grateful to Janet Fisher, Ph.D. for her many thoughtful comments.

We are deeply appreciative of the interest and support of the following friends, family, and colleagues: Janet Stein, M.D., Randye Retkin, Esq., Douglas Feinstein, and Nancy Calcagnini of New York; Christopher and Joanne Gillen of the greater Hartford, Connecticut, area; Sherri Phlaum of the St. Louis, Missouri, area; Mark Goldsmith, M.D., and Annie Goldsmith of the San Francisco Bay area; Thomas Albrecht and Karen Jennings of northern Michigan; and Steven and Donna Stein of the Cleveland, Ohio, area. They provided us with parents and caregivers to interview, shared their personal insights, and in some cases, graciously opened their homes for group discussions.

We are thankful for the love and support of our family and close friends for tolerating our absence and preoccupation, and for enabling our work, at times at their own expense. To Dawn P. Neil, deep gratitude that cannot be expressed with words or salary for her care, attention, and interest.

We also had the good fortune of many other dear friends and colleagues, too numerous to mention, who encouraged us throughout this process. Their kindness, sympathy, and good company sustained us and helped us keep our goal in sight. There were also many strangers in our everyday travels—in coffee shops, at the gym, in bookstores, at the copy center—who showed genuine interest and a curiosity that energized us at crucial moments, strengthening our resolve to see this project through.

We are grateful to Cheryl Houser, Teri Darwish, Felix Kramer and Rochelle Lefkowitz, and Carol McD. Wallace who helped educate and guide us through the strange new world of publishing. To Michael Moskowitz, Ph.D., of Jason Aronson Inc., and to Phyllis Beren, Ph.D., we are grateful for the enthusiasm with which they embraced this work. To Cindy Hyden, acquisitions editor, Elaine Lindenblatt, production editor, and David Kaplan, copy editor, we are deeply appreciative of their guidance, skill, patience, and genuine interest in fine-tuning this manuscript.

Finally, to Linda Neuwirth, C.S.W., friend and colleague, we owe our special gratitude. Her participation early on helped us to explore and expand our theoretical concepts and practical suggestions. Not only did she help to conceive this project, but she generously contributed to its development with sensitivity and wisdom.

Introduction

On street corners and in bookstores, at PTA meetings and in the playground, at gym and music classes, over family dinners, and on the phone and the Internet,[1] parents and caregivers tell their tales of trials and tribulations, frustrations and triumphs. Is this job done for love or for money? This question is a constant refrain that runs through the minds of most working parents and in-home caregivers. By "in-home caregivers" we mean any child care providers working in the home, whether they are called caregivers, nannies, au pairs, babysitters, or housekeepers.

Parents often ruminate over each new, more terrifying, and sensational news report of neglect, abuse, and even murder of children by their caregivers. The most dramatic of these reports was the case of the British au pair, Louise Woodward, whose murder conviction in 1997 was overturned and reduced to involuntary manslaughter.[2] She was sentenced to time served—279 days. Woodward's plight became a media drama and spin war that spanned the Atlantic,[3] roiled the sensibilities[4] of Americans and the British, and reverberated worldwide. This public debate gave voice to parents' unspeakable fears and galvanized extreme feelings about the use of in-home caregivers.[5, 6] In addition, this case put the spotlight on what child care advocates have called a desperate shortage of qualified caregivers for young children.[7]

During this case, facile characterizations abounded of working parents as self-absorbed and relegating their responsibility to unsupervised child care providers. In turn, caregivers were at times portrayed as modern-day slaves, abandoned by parents to manage alone the enormous stressors of day-to-day child care. Global condemnations of caregivers as at best detached and neglectful, and at worst abusive, were made. Like most extreme characterizations, the truth is often somewhere in the middle. Often, it is not as obvious as the screaming headlines and rumor mill might suggest.

We found that most parents and caregivers struggle valiantly with their working relationship. They can often be heard bemoaning their fates, at one extreme, or relishing and idealizing their relationships, at the other. Some parents and caregivers tout their abilities to manage their employees or employers. Others admit to despair in their attempts to do so. But in this most complex relationship employer and employee boundaries are not so neat. These parents and caregivers may feel more like "family," as their lives are inextricably linked. Others may find the relationship difficult or impossible to understand and manage.

WHY STUDY THE RELATIONSHIP BETWEEN PARENTS AND IN-HOME CAREGIVERS?

There is an unmet need to examine what makes these relationships so inherently difficult and what can help them work more smoothly. When the relationship works well, the child has the opportunity to thrive, and parent and caregiver are freer to manage their own complex lives.

Parents and caregivers must balance home and work in a society where working parents are now the norm. The modern nuclear family, consisting of a working father and homemaker mother, has become increasingly replaced by what Edward Shorter [8] has called the "postmodern" family. In this era of the postmodern family, the boundaries, emotional ties, and influences between parents, children, and the general culture have become more fluid and flexible. David Elkind,[9] the noted child psychologist and observer of shifts in the family and its impact on children, has referred to this more fluid and flexible structure as the postmodern permeable family, in which both mother and father work, and children's needs are increasingly met by caregivers.

This expansion of the family boundaries creates a new family "arena" in which emotional ties and influences come to life. Throughout this book, we call this arena the *extended familial space*. We borrow this notion of the extended "space" from D. W. Winnicott,[10] the renowned pediatrician and psychoanalyst. Winnicott first used the term *transitional space* to describe the arena where children's playful illusions of separateness and attachment, autonomy and dependence on their caregivers are lived out and transformed as they grow.

This extended familial space is both a real and a symbolic place. It is both the physical household as well as each member's emotional connection to the people who reside within it. It is a space where the potential for emotional attachments and day-to-day struggles of family life are now expanded to include caregivers, who, by their physical proximity to and intimate involvement in family functions, are inevitably drawn into the family dynamics. Our primary focus here is on understanding and managing this most complex of relationships—the collaborative effort between parents and in-home caregivers.

For many working parents, having a caregiver has many advantages. It gives them more flexibility in their hectic schedules, allows them to pay more individual attention to each child, provides them with consistent child care assistance, and enables them to balance their child care needs, personal needs, and household tasks. But whether child care providers work in the child's own home (in-home caregivers), in the provider's own home (family day care providers), or in day care centers (center day care providers), these arrangements are part of the daily experience and development of most young children. Like the homemaker mother of the 1950s, in-home caregivers, and, to some degree, family day care providers help to anchor a sense of family structure in our postmodern society. Likewise, most center day care providers work to foster a sense of family or "home away from home" in caring for the children in their charge.

This seemingly new expansion of the familial boundaries is really an old approach to an age-old need[11]—help for mothers (and fathers) in the care and rearing of their children. This need had been met in a variety of ways in the past: maiden aunts or orphans, who, as "bound" helpers, lived-in with upper middle class and upper class families; slave mammies, who were child care workers in the antebellum South; and paid nannies and domestic servants, who were part of the American economic expansion in the late nineteenth and early twentieth centuries. Today's parents come to these new child care arrangements with a range of notions about relationships with others of different social classes and cultures. Many of these parents are steeped in egalitarian ideals. They often consciously strive to see their children's caregivers in an equal and collaborative role. Other parents see the relationship as strictly business. These views are also historically familiar. Parents may gravitate toward one or the other of these perspectives for psychological or interpersonal reasons.

In child care and domestic service, money in exchange for employment[12] has, on the surface, helped to maintain a boundary between parents and caregivers. Yet parents and caregivers have described the emotional tugs and struggles in their relationship that invariably arise when one's household and one's most precious attachment (the children) are shared. Money becomes a reminder of the boundaries of the relationship as well as a vehicle for the expression of these inevitable emotional struggles. Most caregivers must contend with the stark reality of low pay, long hours, stress, and isolation. Because these realities are so compelling, they readily become lightning rods for a host of emotional struggles around interpersonal attachment, dependency, and self-esteem.

Children are unfettered by the economics of these arrangements. Most are keenly aware of the presence and emotional meaning of this important person—the caregiver—in their lives. Parents and caregivers may embrace, avoid, or completely discount their meaning and emotional connection to each other. But sharing these core parental functions and attachments to the children cannot help but stir up emotional struggles for parents and caregivers that were forged in their own early family life. The very benefits of having this extended family-like structure can become problematic. The more concretely a caregiver is part of the extended familial space (as is the case with in-home caregivers), the more opportunities there are for intense feelings and conflicts to arise. Similar conflicts and struggles also arise between parents and family day care providers. Caregivers in more institutional settings (day care centers for example) have also described their emotional struggles with parents as well.

Why all the difficulty? Isn't it sufficient for parents and caregivers to operate within an employer and employee structure? Yes, but parents must learn how to set up this working arrangement. Careful background checks, contracts, work responsibilities, pay, vacation schedules, and periodic reviews are all necessary. Finding a caregiver with child care experience, child development training, or certification is crucial, and can help prevent or temper some of the struggles in the relationship.

But even parents who know how to go about employing caregivers are besieged by struggles in the relationship. Parents with managerial expertise, experienced caregivers, and trained child care providers can falter in their attempts to make things work. Anger, fear, jealousy, and resentments can swirl around seemingly simple details of day-to-day living. Old struggles with past relationships and difficult aspects of our own personality are inextricably repeated. What often follows are dramatic crises in which all involved (parents, caregivers, and the children) become engaged in the emotional struggles around loyalty, jealousy, and resentment that typically are reserved for one's own family. A familiar (and familial) refrain was echoed by many of the parents and caregivers that we interviewed about their struggles that ended in terminations, whether planned or unplanned: "It was like getting a divorce."

Focusing on the parent–caregiver relationship as only an employee–employer contract is an attempt to put a rigid frame or boundary on what is inevitably a sticky, unbounded situation. Everyone we interviewed described the ways in which this relationship is like no other. Parents struggle with what to call the caregiver, how to describe her role, their attachment to her, her attachment to them and their child, and their child's attachment to her. They struggle with issues that touch upon the caregiver's value to them in the extended familial space, such as time, money, control, and autonomy. They struggle with transitions and separations, with reunions and termination. So how can one simply be an employer or employee when the work entails the care, safety, nurturance, and development of a child? And how can one help but become like family when working in the intimacy of a household setting or bound up in a family's crucial day-to-day schedules?

Small wonder, then, that hiring and communicating with a caregiver is so difficult. Guidelines, while necessary, are simply not sufficient to make the relationship work. What parents and caregivers have described, and we have evaluated, are ways in which the important emotional and psychological guidelines are ignored. These psychological dynamics are paradoxically obvious, yet covert, accessible, yet warded off by all concerned. It is human nature to fend off our feelings of vulnerability when we need to look at our own role and our own foibles in understanding any interpersonal situation. It is easier to ascribe all the blame and responsibility to others. The relationship between parents and caregivers is no exception to this rule of human dynamics.

The purpose of this book is to assist parents who employ in-home caregivers in knowing more about the psychological and emotional struggles that are inherent in this relationship. While parents live with these day-to-day struggles, they may lack a framework to understand and manage the psychological pulls of this unique arrangement.

This book will also be useful to therapists, teachers, and child care specialists. While more conversant with the psychological framework we offer here, these professionals may not be as familiar with the day-to-day struggles of parents and caregivers. In-home caregivers, particularly those with child care experience and training, family day care providers, and center day care providers may find this book of interest as well, as they assist working parents in their struggles with postmodern family life.

A FRAMEWORK AND GUIDE
FOR THE RELATIONSHIP

The authors' exploration of the parent–caregiver relationship began a number of years ago after receiving a series of phone calls from patients, family, friends, and colleagues who were requesting consultation to discuss various crises that had arisen in their own parent–caregiver relationship. Our work on this subject later evolved into a more focused study.

As we collected thoughts and feelings about these rich experiences, common themes emerged. We illustrate these themes here in a series of vignettes. It is our hope that this approach will communicate the richness and drama of these relationships and the expectations that are often hidden behind seemingly obvious aspects of the employment contract.

Most people we interviewed seemed to be struggling with such issues as pay, schedule, vacations, job requirements, and control. They often had little or no awareness of how these issues symbolized deeper feelings. Because they were confused and overwhelmed, and did not have a framework for understanding their concerns, decisions were often made impulsively. At times abrupt and premature terminations of the relationship resulted, affecting the continuity of care for the children.

Other parents and caregivers seemed to be able to weather various storms, to tolerate differences, and to maintain perspective. They appeared relatively content with the realistic compromises they had chosen to make together in order to make the relationship work.

We believe that the intense feelings and struggles in the relationship are inevitably caused by the expansion of the family boundaries to include the caregiver. This expansion of the boundaries—the extended familial space—offers the potential for a range of adaptive and positive experiences as well struggles and conflicts. The use of this potential hinges on the awareness of the central paradox in this relationship—namely, that while parents and caregiver are technically employer and employee, they also act as if they are an extended family. The extended familial space readily becomes the arena in which feelings of attachment, dependency, idealization, and, at the other extreme, devaluation become the emotional currency. These intense feelings are typically played out around the parents' and caregiver's attempts to negotiate their complex relationship. Since parents create this "space" when they expand the family boundaries, they are ultimately responsible for efforts to make it function as well as possible.

This book is divided into two parts. Part I provides a framework for understanding the relationship between parents and caregivers. Our intent is to bring into focus the central issues that lie at the edge of parents' awareness about their relationship with their caregiver and that the caregiver has in relation to the parents. Many "how to" guides fall short when they fail to set the framework for understanding the phenomena under discussion. Following such concrete guides is a little like acting a part in a play without knowing your character's motivations, or like learning dance steps without the rhythm of the beat or the passion of the music. Chapter 1 describes how caregivers have become an integral part of the contemporary household for many working parents. We note the potential for the roles of parents and caregivers to overlap in the extended familial space. This space is an extension of the maternal and paternal functions that arise when the family boundaries are broadened to include the caregiver. This overlap can create conflicting expectations, causing confusion and conflict. We describe this confusion and conflict as the central paradox that we mentioned above. While most parents and caregivers speak openly of this paradox, they often are unaware of how these emotionally compelling forces can inform their day-to-day attempts to be employer and employee. Chapter 2 broadly addresses the cultural context of changes in the roles of parents and the family structure, and the history of the caregiving of the children of working parents. (We note the universal nature of the intense feelings and related struggles that arise in the care of children and extend this notion to include the in-home caregiver.) Chapter 3 describes how parents and caregivers often experience their relationship in extremes, from idealization to devaluation. We note that feelings of dependency and needs for care and nurturance are at the core of these extreme views, and often fuel conflicts in the relationship. In this context we present a particularly relevant aspect of child development—the attachment to and separation from parents and primary caregivers. Chapter 4 probes the challenges in managing the boundaries of this important relationship of parents and caregivers. We discuss in depth two seemingly obvious but central themes from the interviews—that in this paradoxical "as if" relationship between parents and caregiver, the caregiver moves along a constantly shifting continuum from employee to family member; and that the exchange of money has both real and symbolic meaning with unofficial and official components. Chapter 5 is a guide to the process of noting and exploring the multiple meanings often lying outside of the awareness of parents and caregivers in the struggles that can arise in the relationship. Real aspects of the arrangements can stir up connections to earlier times, old relationships, and past struggles for both parents and caregivers. We note that these struggles from the past can frequently be enacted dramatically in the present, typically outside the awareness of the participants.

Part II provides a guide for managing the relationship between parents and caregivers, including practical help in beginning a relationship and in dealing with the inevitable ups and downs. We also examine how endings are typically negotiated and what parents and caregivers may struggle with in this phase of the relationship. Chapter 6 deals with the core attributes that parents and caregivers look for in each other as well as more individual needs and expectations, conscious or unconscious. Unconscious needs and expectations exert a potent presence and inform the nature of the ongoing relationship (and the termination phase as well). We present three steps in our guide to establishing the good-enough relationship: (1) a child care needs assessment, (2) the do's and don'ts of interviewing, and (3) how to detect a good match with a caregiver. Chapter 7 presents a guide for establishing and maintaining a good-enough relationship between parents and caregivers. We describe two crucial aspects of this ongoing collaborative process: (1) how to foster mutual communication, and (2) how to develop an extended familial space—a genuine stance of mutual concern and caregiving in the relationship. The subject of termination is discussed in Chapter 8. We outline the range of possible finales to the relationship: emergency terminations, unplanned endings, and planned endings. We enumerate ways to spot a less than good-enough relationship and child care arrangement using signals from parents, the caregiver, and the children. We describe situations in which ongoing unconscious dynamics can lead to crisis and precipitous terminations, which are the most difficult for all concerned. We note that while all terminations are stressful, those that are planned and approached with the needs of all considered offer the best possibilities for adaptation and growth regarding a crucial and lifelong stressor—dealing with separation and loss. Chapter 9 summarizes and extends our observations.

OUR STUDY APPROACH

When we describe our interview process as a *study*, we mean very specifically a careful examination or analysis[13] of a phenomenon. We worked to establish an open dialogue with a total of eighty-five people who were intimately involved with core aspects of the parent–caregiver relationship. These individual and group sessions were primarily with parents and in-home caregivers, but also home day care providers, center day care providers, and child care employment agency personnel. Interview sessions were between 1 and 2 hours long, and in some cases, follow-up sessions were held. We conducted the interviews ourselves, and listened with a clinical "ear" as psychoanalysts to the answers to our open-ended questions. This approach allowed us to explore the deeper issues and feelings that seemed to characterize the relationship between parents and caregivers. We explored aspects of the communication process, job functions and role expectations, stressors, adaptations, and conceptualization of the relationship. Our professional experiences, along with examples offered by colleagues, helped to round out the emerging picture of the multifaceted relationship between parents and caregivers. We reviewed examples of parents' attempts in psychotherapy to grapple with a range of emotional reactions, struggles, and misidentifications of current interpersonal situations because of feelings from their past—expectations, needs, longing, and mixed feelings related to their own childhood experiences—now enacted in struggles with caregivers. Our more casual observations of and exchanges with parents and caregivers in natural settings such as the playground, at the bus stop, at enrichment classes, and in the schools also allowed for organizing familiar themes and formulating our ideas about the relationship—particularly what works and what doesn't and why. Finally, our personal experiences with the parent–caregiver relationship, as well as our own clinical and theoretical frame, helped to organize our observations and create a framework to conceptualize the good-enough relationship and a guide to managing it well. We fully recognize that this is a qualitative look and not an exhaustive study of the relationship between parents and caregivers, let alone the complex issues of child care in general. Yet our view of the essence of the relationship comes from a condensation of a wide range of data.

A "good-enough" relationship between parents and caregivers is one in which there is a conscious agreement to collaborate toward providing a good-enough child care arrangement, one in which there is a primary focus on, and commitment to, the care of children. This requires that parents and caregivers use all of their positive childhood experiences, informal learning, and formal training about child care and child development to stay attuned to the rapidly changing needs of the growing child. "Good enough" also refers to things working this way more times than not.

Our interviews were conducted with only women caregivers since they make up the vast majority of in-home caregivers (and home and center day care providers as well). While most of the interviews were a convenience sample, a number of interviews were conducted with caregivers and parents solicited from or referred by physician's offices and caregiver employment agencies. These interviews were primarily conducted in New York City, but the sample also included individual and group interviews in the suburban New York metropolitan tristate area, and in Midwest and West Coast urban/suburban areas. An attempt was made to strike a balance in the interviews between family–caregiver arrangements in which things seemed to be working well and those in which there was a more conscious awareness of some crisis or ongoing difficulty. Included were cases of in-home caregivers who had been terminated or had voluntarily left a family (interviewed separately from and in addition to the parents).

The parents in this sample were primarily middle and upper middle class working professional parents with one or more young children. The caregivers were primarily immigrants from a number of Caribbean, South American, European, and Asian countries. Many had children of their own, either with them in the United States or at home in their native land, typically in the care of relatives. Most of the caregivers had previous childcare experience or had reared their own children. The caregivers who were mothers themselves were also asked about their experiences with the people, often relatives, caring for their own children. Some of these caregivers, in particular the family day care providers and center day care providers, had formal training courses in child development, child care, home health care, or nursing.

An important window into the types of relationships and the nature of ongoing struggles that can develop between parents and in-home caregivers was created during the interviews themselves. Most people were initially either extremely interested in or wary about being interviewed or having their employer or employee interviewed. Some parents seemed resistant to any notion that they hadn't figured it all out, as our interest in the relationship seemed to imply to them. There was a sense that a balance had been struck and that they were wary of upsetting the relationship. Most parents and caregivers were genuinely aware of issues with which they grappled, and were eager to share their experiences in the context of what we had learned. People seemed to need to talk about their concerns, and in many cases we ran out of time before they ran out of interest. Our interview seemed to help them identify core issues and to use these insights in their own negotiation of this complex relationship.

A FEW POINTS OF CLARIFICATION

When we refer to caregivers in this book, we mean specifically in-home caregivers, such as nannies, au pairs, babysitters, and housekeepers. When we refer to other types of caregiver arrangements, such as family day care or center day care, we will so specify. We do this not only to simplify our discussion but to highlight the degree of overlap that exists in the relational dynamics described by parents and caregivers in these various settings.

Our intention is not to evaluate or endorse the effectiveness of the in-home caregiver as a child care arrangement, but to provide a way of conceptualizing the relationship so that it works best for all involved. This arrangement has become a child care option for many busy parents for a variety of sociocultural, economic, and personal reasons. It is beyond the scope of this book to examine these complex factors in detail. However, it is our belief, and most child care experts would likely agree, that a collaborative relationship between parents and their child care providers is a crucial component of all quality child care arrangements.

The vignettes that form the core of this book came from the experiences of the parents and caregivers observed and interviewed, and from the experiences of the authors and their colleagues. While names, occupations, and specific details have been changed, and while some cases are composites, the essence of the stories has been preserved.

A final word: Many parents may give lip service to the notion that a caregiver is "just like a member of the family," but this is no simple matter. As we point out, successful relationships are complex and require tremendous effort and forbearance.

PART I

UNDERSTANDING THE PARENT–CAREGIVER RELATIONSHIP

1

For Love or Money?

"It was the worst day of my life. I questioned every single decision I ever made."

This was the way that one mother, Ellen, began her interview. She was describing an experience that she had as she prepared for the first full week of employment of Diana, her infant son's caregiver, an in-home child care provider. At the time, Sam was 3½ months old. Diana had been working half days for two weeks prior to her transition to a full-time schedule.

It was a hectic and emotionally difficult time for Ellen. She was arranging for her own return to full-time work. This meant leaving little Sam in Diana's full-time care. Ellen forgot to make a set of keys to her home for Diana on this last day before the transition to full-time work for them both. Ellen kept her own set of keys when she left to run an errand and Diana took Sam out for a walk in the park. She told Diana to be back at the house at one o'clock. When Ellen returned at the agreed time, neither child nor caregiver was there.

For over an hour, Ellen felt "tormented" by worries of what might have happened to Sam. She wondered what sort of woman she had chosen to care for her child. She questioned her own judgment as well as Diana's. She began to fear her son had been kidnapped, maimed, or killed in some horrible accident. She felt frightened, guilty, and enraged: "I was paralyzed with emotions." Ellen finally tracked them down through Cynthia, the woman who had glowingly recommended Diana. Diana was a friend of Cynthia and her children's caregiver. Diana and Sam had gone to Cynthia's home after the park. When Ellen questioned Diana, she simply said that Sam had fallen asleep, and she didn't want to wake him, "just to get back at one o'clock." Looking back at this experience, Ellen noted: "At that moment, I had to accept the fact that I would have to relinquish some of my power over my child to someone else. I had to let go."

After a discussion with her husband, Jed, Ellen decided to continue on with Diana as Sam's caregiver. The quality of care that was evident early on and the deep level of their attachment have justified the "gut feeling" Ellen had when she first met Diana and decided to hire her. "We have a loving relationship," Ellen said. As Ellen reflected during the years upon this frightening experience, she concluded, "Diana was trying to tell me that *she* was going to be in charge in some ways, that *she* was the nanny or 'day mother.'" Yet as she spoke about their relationship in the present, it seemed that the initial conflict over "control" of the daily routine continues to reveal itself as a focal point in their relationship.

We can only imagine the depth of anxiety and panic for this mother, Ellen, when her son Sam and his new caregiver Diana didn't show up as expected. Television, radio, newspapers, and movies offer constant reminders of the potential dangers for children that seem to lurk around every corner. Terrifying news reports of nannies and caregivers who have neglected, abused, and even killed the children in their care can easily become lightning rods for the fears of working parents like Ellen. If we add to this mix Ellen's own understandable maternal struggles with separating from little Sam, we can understand how such panic situations can arise.

We can also empathize with Ellen's focus on control as a central issue in the relationship as she returned to her own full-time work and turned Sam over to Diana. Ellen's difficulty with making a set of keys for Diana at this stressful time of transition was surely more than an oversight by a busy working mother about to return to work. It was a symbol rife with personal meaning that captured her struggle with handing over access to her household and daytime control of Sam in her physical absence.

Diana, too, herself a working mother, had struggles over leaving her own child in day care. She had her own ideas and experience in caring for babies. She was moving into her new role in this household as a substitute for mother, for Ellen—in charge of the moment-to-moment care of Sam in this capacity, including decisions regarding comings and goings. Yet Diana had been less than sensitive to her new employer's anxieties as a mother leaving her own child with another mother. Diana had also forgotten the decorum of being a new employee who should be "playing by the rules."

In one of the discussion groups that we held for working parents with children in the care of nannies, au pairs, and caregivers, a mother was forced to confront a similar and ongoing difficulty with handing over the keys to her child's nanny. This mother described her concern for security as the reason that the nanny wasn't allowed to hold onto her own set of keys. Instead, the nanny was given her own special place to leave the keys each day. Another mother in the group was so startled by this complicated and seemingly illogical arrangement that she blurted out what was to her an obvious but, likely, a painful reality: "You trust her with your kids, but not with a set of keys to your house?"

In a sense, this symbol of control—the keys—was a concrete expression of this difficult struggle. But such struggles over control are just a small part of the inherent dilemma and contradiction faced by thousands of working mothers.

THE CENTRAL PARADOX

This mother, Ellen, and her children's nanny, Diana, as well as Jed and little Sam, were all sharing in these moments a central paradox in their interrelationship. Caregivers are, in one sense, employees. Yet somehow this label fails to capture the richness and emotional impact of their day-to-day presence in the homes of working parents. Caregivers can also feel more like "family," entrusted with the crucial day-to-day care, safety, and welfare of parents' most precious attachments—their children.

The typical questions that understandably arise for most mothers and fathers shed some light on this central paradox: "Is this person doing this for love, like a mother, with a bond of feeling, concern, and attachment, or only for money, simply like any employee?" To allow for the development of a hoped-for bond between caregiver and child, mothers like Ellen have to expand the household space to include not only a caregiver's physical presence, but also her psychological and emotional presence as well—just like an extended family member. Yet there is this nagging contradiction here that continues to make its presence known. While both parents and caregivers often experience each other "as if" they were family to one another, all the while they know on some level that they are not really family but rather employer and employee. Most parents and caregivers speak of this "familial" pull, but are unaware of just how often it can inform the inevitable struggles in the relationship.

In many ways, the caregiver must function at certain times as if she were a family member, tending to the personal needs of the child, such as feeding, changing, soothing, and stimulating in an age-appropriate way. These functions are essentially the same ones that mother, father, and extended family members perform in mother's absence. An essential ingredient of a successful parent–caregiver relationship is the caregiver's capacity to adapt to the family's way of doing things as well as the parents' ability to allow for it to happen. The caregiver must be able to fit in and blend with the family, to become a member, as if she were a part of the family. Success of this as-if quality depends on a flexible ability to suspend reality to some degree—at times overlooking the fact that she is technically an employee.

In some ways this is not unlike an adult version of the play acting that children do when they pretend to be a princess, a superhero, or simply mommy, daddy, or baby. In this play, they "become" the person they pretend to be, deeply attached to and immersed in their role. All the while, they are also aware of who they really are. But they can quickly take a break to have a snack or become upset with a playmate and need some adult comfort, slipping easily in and out of roles.

It is the very awareness and acknowledgment of this paradoxical arrangement, unlike any other employee–employer relationship, that allows for this creative suspension of reality. By this we mean that the caregiver's role as employee can then be expanded as if she is family, allowing for the infant or child to attach to the caregiver as a substitute for mother (in her absence). One in-home caregiver described it this way:

> At the end of the day, you're still an employee. But while you're there, you do fill the "space" of a parent. And I am sort of friends with the parents, too—it just kind of happened over time, I don't know how exactly. Somewhere along the way they started to ask me about myself and I answered. Then I started to offer things myself. You *do* get attached.

When the caregiver enters the household space each morning, she makes a crucial transition to this as-if role of both employee and extended family. This complex transition requires its own space and time to develop. Many parents underestimate the importance of these moments of transition, understandably, as they rush to meet early morning schedules and work responsibilities. However, symbolically the reins are being handed over to the caregiver in these pivotal moments. The ways in which these moments of transition are negotiated by parents and caregivers can be a potent source of conflicts, and reflect parents' and caregivers' own struggles with these overlapping, yet unique roles.

Janice, the mother of 2-year-old Emma, described her mixed feelings in these crucial moments of transition with Emma's caregiver, Sally:

> When I'm ready to go out the door to work and Sally comes in, my impulse is to run—it can feel easier for me, for Emma, for everyone, but it ends up worse in the long run. I make a conscious effort to give Sally the basics—how did Emma sleep, eat, make a BM [bowel movement], anything cute or unusual, the day's schedule. But I know that this stuff is more than the basics. I can feel myself letting go of the mother role and almost handing it over, not that I'm not still preoccupied with Emma all day, but that's the reality of it. If I can't do that, how can I expect Sally to do her job, for me to do mine when I'm away at work, and how can Emma feel that Sally is really there? I won't kid you. It rips at me emotionally sometimes, both when Emma is all clinging—a *terrible two* extraordinaire she is right now—and when I see her happy as a clam holding Sally's hand and waving goodbye, that's bittersweet, too. Such mixed feelings.

When a mother and father leave in the morning or the caregiver leaves or retires for the evening, or at drop-off and pick-up times at family or center day care, there needs to be some discussion not only of the scheduling details, but also of the day-to-day emotional and psychological needs and interests of the child. To fail to do this is to treat the unique and yet overlapping roles of parents and caregivers as a merely functional relationship, that is, as simply employer and employee. But the struggles and reluctance to hand over the reins that can occur when parents leave for work or when caregivers take their leave at the end of the day is another extreme in the relationship in which caregivers may feel too much like family. In such moments, the as-if quality of this unique relationship is lost.

Janice described parallel needs and expectations of Emma's caregiver, Sally, at the end of the day.

> When I come back, I expect the same from Sally, the same kind of information and consideration so I can pick up from there. If Sally is too tight-lipped, or can't be bothered because she's in her own rush, it only sets me up for failure. It's like the missing piece is with Sally and she's gone off with it. I mean we're not changing shifts at the 7-Eleven!

This transitional time and space was described by center day care providers as well. A kind of neutral area seemed to be used by some to play out the very charged feelings about the overlapping boundaries that exist between parents and caregivers. Here's how one center day care provider described the intense drama of this seemingly perfunctory transition:

> There are spots in the day care rooms where the mothering and fathering things go on, like feeding, changing, or the rocking chair. For some parents, for us to be in those spaces with the kids while they are there becomes uncomfortable. Some parents are comfortable only if I take the child from them in these neutral spots—like where they play with a pile of toys. So we do it gradually or indirectly. It's a dance, and if choreographed well, you don't step on anyone's toes.

Another sensitive caregiver described it this way:

> I just don't reach over and take the child when I come in. I wait for them to present the child to me, because that's when they're ready. There is a lot behind reaching over to take the child. It's not such a simple thing. I've learned by my mistakes. I've learned to say, "Whenever you're ready, I'll be over here." Whatever I need to know about the previous night, I wait for the parents to tell me first, to give them a chance. Then I only need to ask if I need to know.

Some parents seem to have particular difficulty in making these transitions. One mother described an ongoing struggle with the notion that someone else, the caregiver, was moving into this space with her son:

> I would always make a point of reminding her [the caregiver] of exactly what time to arrive in the morning since my schedule was always changing. I was very explicit. But she would come 10 or sometimes 15 minutes early. And I grew to resent it. Like, this was my time with Mark, so why are you here?

Where this delicate balance, this central paradox of roles for caregivers and parents, often breaks down is when the participants—mother, father, caregiver, and child—fail to read each other properly. To forget that this is an as-if relationship in which the caregiver is paradoxically both employee and extended family is a potential source of conflict and ongoing stress in these child care relationships.

For one mother, Susan, this delicate balance seemed to break down when her child's caregiver, Nina, seemed so much like family that Susan felt compelled to take care of Nina in a way that went beyond the immediate situation and echoed old struggles of her own. Nina had developed serious personal problems at home. She wanted Susan, an attorney, to help her obtain a divorce. Nina had become emotionally upset at work at times. Susan's child, Mike, had been exposed to a number of phone calls in which Nina cried, was angry, and spoke of her difficulties with relatives and friends.

Susan decided it would be in everyone's best interest to have Mike begin a longer day program in nursery school. Her son loved his half days there and very much wanted this. Susan thought it would protect him from Nina's mood swings at this difficult time. In addition, it would also alleviate her worries about getting to work on time since her own schedule had suffered.

Susan was preoccupied with Nina's trouble and emotional state to the point that she became concerned about taking Mike away from Nina when Nina was so upset. Susan said, "I feel intense guilt because 95 percent of the time I think of my child and myself first and not of her." While this would commonly be viewed as appropriate, Susan seemed truly disturbed at the thought of putting her own needs first. Reflecting upon her feelings of guilt, which at face value made no sense, Susan realized that she had frequently had the same feelings toward her own mother that she now had about the caregiver, Nina. Recognizing this, she could then understand that she had been relating to Nina as if Nina were her own mother, who needed Susan's help, a role that Susan had often assumed for her mother.

Once aware that these feelings were out of place (or displaced, we might say), Susan understood that her guilt was inappropriate to this present situation. This feeling was, in great part, old baggage. Susan's self-reflection helped her to set her priorities straight, realizing that she was, first and foremost, responsible for her child's needs being best served. Armed with this new, more balanced perspective with Nina as a person, an employee, but like an extended family member, Susan could better manage the situation to everyone's advantage.

Parents often expect the kind of care, loyalty, and devotion from the caregiver that family might ideally provide. At the same time, they may resent some of the very attachment to their children that these kinds of familial bonds offer. Caregivers likewise expect certain boundaries for their work schedule, pay, and autonomy. But they may also expect special flexibility given this central paradox in which their presence and central importance in the home is not only a job requirement but a necessity for child care. Some caregivers, particularly those who leave their own families in a foreign land, may wish and expect that they will, in turn, be embraced as family.

CAREGIVERS: ONE ADAPTATION
TO THE CHILD CARE CRISIS

The modern nuclear family of the 1950s, consisting of a working father and a homemaker mother, is a rapidly fading image.[1] This traditional domestic arrangement now represents less than one-quarter of all United States households with children.[2] Currently, in nearly 75 percent of all households with children, both parents (or the primary parent in single-parent households) are working. This shift reflects dramatic changes in family structure, household tasks, and the workplace over the past three decades.[3]

As working parents grapple with the difficult task of finding appropriate child care in the face of these enormous societal shifts in the home and the workplace, in-home caregivers (nannies, au pairs, babysitters), home child care providers, and center day care providers have become an integral, functioning aspect of the contemporary family household. Recent U.S. Census Bureau data indicate that when mothers work outside the home, their children's caregivers are most likely to be nonrelatives, either in homes or in day care centers.[4] While relatives currently care for nearly half of the estimated ten million preschoolers with mothers employed outside the home, the balance is cared for either by in-home caregivers and home day care providers (22 percent) or by center day care providers (30 percent).

We seem to know intuitively that infants and children thrive on consistent and individual attention. Children develop best when they have a balance of new experiences in the context of what is familiar to them, a solid home base, so to speak. It makes sense, then, that a warm, consistent, and attentive caregiver, well known to parent and child, available in a familiar setting, would potentially provide for the best care.[5] Working parents tend to prefer such flexible home-like child care arrangements for their children.[6] There is some support for the notion that such "individual" attention is associated with good care.

A recent national child care study conducted by the National Institute of Child Health and Human Development indicates that for working parents the highest-quality child care is typically provided by relatives (fathers and grandparents), and in-home caregivers because of the one-on-one attention available.[7] Other national studies of center and home day care conducted in the 1980s have shown that caregivers who are trained in child development tend to relate to and interact with children with more constructive and age-appropriate responses that are individualized to their needs.[8] Recent research by Susan Kontos, director of the Center for Families at Purdue University, into the components of quality child care in day care homes and centers confirms both of these findings; a low number of children per child care provider (i.e., more individual attention) is associated with more frequent interactions between child and caregiver.[9] The research emphasizes that such quality care is a function of a caregiver's experience with, understanding of, and most importantly training in, child development. Kontos and her colleagues summarized their key findings as follows: "Both parents and caregivers see a warm, caring, responsive relationship between the child and the provider, a safe environment, and good communications between parent and provider as the crux of quality." All of these factors are seen as essential in assuring that a caregiver's individual attention fosters good development. In this regard, a number of caregiver training programs and certifications in early child care have been developed under the auspices of organizations such as the National Association for the Education of Young Children,[10] the National Association for Family Child Care,[11] as well as through various collaborations between public agencies and corporate sponsors. Recently, a national effort has been unveiled to address the desperate need for qualified and affordable child care providers.[12]

Thus, many parents feel, and most professionals would likely agree, that consistent availability of reliable, warm, experienced, and trained caregivers is a central aspect of any quality child care arrangement.[13] The in-home caregiver arrangement is often viewed as potentially optimal in this way by working parents who come to this caregiver arrangement for help in balancing their own hectic lives and irregular work schedules. Ironically, this potentially ideal child care arrangement for working parents poses certain problems and struggles in the relationship between parents and caregivers.[14]

We have found that in some cases typical struggles around cultural differences in child-rearing approaches, the degree of autonomy that caregivers are allowed, feelings of jealousy, and degree of attachment and dependency that arise in the relationship may be due in part to a caregiver's lack of formal child care training. Parents who can afford the additional expense often address their caregiver's lack of training by enrolling them early on in classes for infants or children and caregivers, and then move the children into early preschool. This helps to improve the quality of care and can also help to reduce the conflicts between parents and caregivers to some degree. However, studies of trained family day care providers and center day care providers have also noted that the relations between providers and parents can at times become intense and conflictual.[15] Struggles can result when attempts are made to collaborate with parents around issues such as toilet training, discipline, providing structure in the home, and developmental problems that might be noted. Some parents are threatened by a caregiver's training or certification, feeling that they know the child best, particularly when facing the narcissistic blow of a child who seems to be lagging behind his peers in terms of developmental milestones.

The individual characteristics, interpersonal exchanges, and relationship between parents and caregivers have been increasingly viewed as a missing link in understanding what constitutes quality child care.[16] The infant researcher Sally Provence[17] has concluded that it is the active collaboration, the working relationship between parents and child care providers, that is the key to success or failure in these child care arrangements. Susan Kontos and her colleagues also acknowledged the importance of caregivers' relationships with parents in their study of quality child care.[18] They asked family day care providers and relative day care providers a series of questions about typical areas of conflict, their degree of interrelationship (i.e., sharing personal time or information), and general communication about the children in their care. Not surprisingly, a range of positive and negative experiences was described. Most of the child care providers socialized with the parents, shared feelings, and talked about their own lives and their own children. A third of the nonrelative day care providers considered the parents to be friends. Arguments were typically centered on disagreements about child-rearing practices, money, and the schedule, particularly the difficult transition times of drop off and pick up.

Over the past three decades, several important historical works have examined the significance and impact of caregivers from historical, social, economic, and cultural perspectives. Jonathan Gathhorne-Hardy offers a fascinating treatment of the British nanny in *The Unnatural History of the Nanny*.[19] Through a vast array of data that includes interviews with nannies, biographical descriptions of historical figures, and historical, economic, and literary references, he analyzed the meaning and impact of the nanny as a British institution. He describes a range of working relationships between mothers and nannies. Some nannies took total control of their children (as they referred to them). Mothers would quietly acquiesce, only to appear on the scene when the children were 5 or 6 years old. Other nannies and mothers seemed to have more of a partnership, a collaborative effort toward sharing the work of child rearing.

On this side of the Atlantic, Faye E. Dudden's *Serving Women: Household Service in Nineteenth Century America*,[20] using a wide range of memoirs, literary sources, and historical data, documented the complex social roles of women as employees and employers. She notes that the tenor of the relationship between domestic servants, child care workers, and the families with whom they lived ranged from the intensely personal to the thoroughly businesslike. In *Telling Memories Among Southern Women: Domestic Workers and their Employers in the Segregated South*, Susan Tucker[21] documented the complex emotions and bonds between the races through the oral histories of women employers and domestic workers. Geraldine Youcha's *Minding the Children*[22] spans both continents in her comprehensive study of the history of child care in America with its roots in the European apprenticeship system. She makes a compelling argument for the notion that throughout time, and certainly throughout American history, child care has always been a shared endeavor among women and extended family.

A more recent comprehensive sociological look at the phenomena of in-home child care was addressed by Julia Wrigley in her book, *Other People's Children*.[23] Wrigley described important social and socioeconomic issues in the working arrangement of parents and caregivers such as class differences and potential exploitation of workers by some employers. While Wrigley noted that personality factors play a large part in struggles that can arise in these working relationships, her book left unexplored the underlying psychological factors and dynamic issues that are inherent to this child care arrangement. Susan Cheever's compelling look at the work history or "nanny track"[24] of one New York caregiver touched upon a number of the day-to-day struggles in the lives of caregivers and working parents who paradoxically go off to work and hire others to care for their children. Stacey Schiff's look at the mother–caregiver relationship from both a personal and a literary vantage point, "The Runaway Mother,"[25] captured some of the emotional ups and downs that are often glossed over, perhaps simply because they are often too painful to acknowledge head on.

We believe that what makes or breaks the relationship between parents and caregivers is the ability of parents and caregivers to understand and manage this paradox, the overlapping parental or familial function and the role as employee that caregivers occupy. The quality of their working relationship affects not only the psychological well-being of each party but also the development of the child. Children know when relations are strained between the parents. It makes intuitive sense that they detect these struggles between parents and their caregivers as well, however subtle they may seem.

An experience of one of our colleagues seemed to capture the degree to which this complex and emotionally charged relationship between caregivers and parents has been overlooked and underestimated even by mental health professionals. In our interview, she described a discussion with a friend and senior colleague about her distress and sense of guilt over the serious illness of her son's caregiver. She related her exchange with her friend, a sensitive and learned psychologist and psychoanalyst: "If only I had pushed her [the caregiver] to have more frequent physical exams, maybe this would have been detected and treated earlier." The response from her colleague spoke volumes: "What else could you do? You're not her mother, after all!"

For this parent at this moment in the relationship, it was as if the caregiver were part of the family. She was expressing a feeling of connection to the caregiver in her extended family role while simultaneously aware of her importance as an employee.

Clearly, the relationships that evolve between parents and caregivers are intense, complex, and multifaceted. The very essence of these relationships often leads to situations of danger. It can create interpersonal and dynamic points of conflict for all. Conflicts pertaining to basic issues of trust, loyalty, dependency, loving, and hating can become revived from the past. They are then reexperienced in new and complicated versions as the household space is expanded to include the physical and psychological presence of the caregiver.

It is no surprise, then, that most parents and caregivers experience mixed feelings or ambivalence toward one another. Often, aspects of their ambivalence is experienced simultaneously. For example, for mothers, the following wishes might exist side by side: "I want to [need to] work" and "I want to [need to] stay home with my young child." For the caregivers, parallel feelings exist. Many caregivers are working mothers themselves. They leave their own families—sometimes in another country with other caregivers—to care for other people's children. Paradoxically, the success of their performance depends on their capacity to attach themselves to another child. They are also called on to manage their sadness connected with the fact that these children in their care are not their own.

These mixed feelings are common and can potentially cause distress and conflict when parents and caregivers are unaware of or unable to acknowledge them. Messages such as "Be close, loving, and concerned" (i.e., be like family) are typically countered with, "Don't replace me with my child" (i.e., just be an employee). From the caregiver's standpoint, the message is: "Don't interfere with the special and unique bond I may have with this child for whom I expend so much time and energy." Negotiating all of these boundaries is a complex but important task. How do parents and caregivers manage to successfully negotiate all these potential land mines?

For each person, sorting out appropriate expectations (emotional as well as practical) of the other is indeed a formidable task. Anxieties often center around raw and painful emotions connected with fears such as dependency and abandonment—feelings that we all resist knowing yet, paradoxically, need to be aware of in order to live fully and effectively in the moment. So for the mother, painful anxieties and fears may be echoed in an internal dialogue such as this: "Will my caregiver quit?" "Will my child love her better than she loves me?" "Will my child hate me for leaving her each day I go to work?" For the caregiver, parallel anxieties can exist: "Will my employer fire me if I connect too much or too little with this child?" "How will my own children manage their envy of the children I work with?" It can be a confusing and overwhelming situation. All parties in this shared endeavor must accept that the parents are ultimately in charge. At the same time, both parents and caregivers need to oversee and safeguard this delicate balance—letting bonds develop and autonomy be fostered while real boundaries are never forgotten.

2

Defining the Boundaries

At a recent holiday dinner with a large, extended Italian-American family, one of the authors discussed what has become the hot family topic of the 1990s: Who best cares for children? There was a range of experience and opinion about whether or not both parents should work and leave their children with a caregiver. One married couple with two teenage daughters had decided that the mother, Catherine, would stay at home until the children were in their teens before she returned to work full time. As a nurse, she had done some part-time work while the girls were growing, but it was minimal. Another couple had decided to have home child care while both went to work. Their children, now in school, continue to have the same caregiver. One set of grandparents had been opposed on principle to this arrangement and had spoken their disapproval over the years. The question of which parents loved their children more was often tossed about and heatedly discussed from the various perspectives. As we reflected on the way the two sets of children had developed, even the grandparents admitted that, contrary to their fears, their grandchildren who were left with a caregiver had not suffered from this arrangement. Although they wanted to hold onto their belief system, they could not argue with success!

Another working mother in the family, Gloria, was not present at this gathering. Her only child, Sally, had died

from a congenital metabolic disease at an early age, causing
tremendous sorrow to her parents and to the entire family.
The grandparents looked more open-mindedly upon the
question of parental love and the choice (and need) of both
parents to work outside the home, thanks, in part, to a
sensitive and insightful reflection by Catherine, the mother
who returned to work after her children were in their teens.
Catherine told the grandparents, "I understood why Gloria
decided to go back to work when Sally was born. Gloria
never shared the sad news of Sally's genetic disorder, but
I knew there was something wrong. What would Gloria do
when Sally died? She had to go back to work for her own
sanity and for Sally's—however long she would live!"
Catherine shared these thoughts in an effort to help her
in-laws understand that there was no simple or single right
approach. In a subsequent conversation, Gloria corrected
Catherine's opinion as to why she had gone back to work.
"I always intended to go back to work because I wanted to
work as well as have a child—not because I needed to work
simply as solace to distract me from my daughter's condition."

In *A Mother's Place*, Susan Chira[1] makes precisely this
point. Woman want to work for varied and complex reasons. She argues intelligently and reasonably that a
mother's happiness and satisfaction have a more profound,
lasting effect on her children than whether or not she works
outside the home. In addition to deep emotional tugs and
pulls, this question of who best cares for children, mothers
who stay at home or mothers who work outside the home,
provokes intense emotions and touches upon the enormous
changes in the family over the last three decades.

THE FAMILY OF THE 1990s AND
THE EXTENDED FAMILIAL SPACE

An enormous social revolution has been unfolding in this
country and throughout the world since the 1960s as noted

in the emergence of new family structures. There is a wave of nostalgia in America for the modern nuclear family, epitomized by 1950s TV shows like "Ozzie and Harriet," our cultural ideal of the homemaker mother and breadwinner father. We seem to be longing to reestablish this ideal image of the nuclear family unit in order to cope with uncertainties about roles and expectations in these shifts to the new postmodern family.

In her book, *In the Name of the Family*, sociologist Judith Stacey[2] notes that the household structure that has come the closest to replacing the modern nuclear family, both normatively and culturally, is the working married couple with children. She cites economic realities as well as the impact of feminism on our culture as two central factors in this shift. Related factors such as the dramatic rise in the divorce rate and the high frequency of remarriage and blended families has created an even greater diversity of family patterns. She states, "In an era when most married mothers are employed, when women perform most working-class jobs, when most occupations are unorganized and fail to pay a family wage, when marriage links are tenuous and transitory, and when more single women than married homemakers are rearing children, conventional notions of a normal working-class family no longer make sense. . . . Stereotypes are moral (alas, more often, immoral) stories people tell to organize the complexity of social experience" (pp. 30–31). Simply stated, we live in a society where family "stories" are diverse and multiple.

In his book, *The Ties That Stress: The New Family Imbalance*, psychologist David Elkind,[3] professor of child study at Tufts University, explores in depth the postmodern family that has emerged in this country in the last two decades. Unlike the modern nuclear family of the 1950s that had an imbalance of needs weighted in favor of the children over parents, especially mothers, this postmodern family is imbalanced in favor of the needs of the parents over the children. He points out that both family types are out of balance and that whenever one group meets its needs at the expense of another, stress and conflict result.

The myth of the nuclear family as the most highly evolved, progressive structure for family living has also been challenged on various fronts. Elkind reminds us of the prevalence and impact of disturbances created within the emotional ties of the idealized modern nuclear family such as family violence, physical and emotional neglect and abuse, scapegoating, and emotional belittling. He notes that the myth of the ideal nuclear family unit has also been undermined by the astronomical rise in the divorce rate, the high incidence of depression among mothers, and the increased prevalence of physical symptoms in children related to psychosocial stressors.

Elkind also addresses the inherent limitations of the new imbalanced family where the needs of working parents are placed in the forefront. He notes that factors such as the loss of privacy when others are included in the familial space, the implicit belief that working mothers should still be primarily responsible for housework and child care, and a minimizing of the differences between parents and children are sources of stress and disequilibrium.

Elkind believes that this new imbalanced family has its pluses as well. While the role of parents as breadwinner and homemaker ensured that children's needs for protection and guidance would be met, today's postmodern permeable family with its particular structure teaches children, for example, the skills of organization and self-discipline, basic for survival in today's world. It also enables women to develop their potential in the workplace and learn the necessary skills and experience to be self-supporting, if that should become necessary.

Elkind recognizes that since "abuse and neglect may be

as frequent in nuclear families as love, protection and commitment are in nonnuclear families, . . . [what is] crucial to effective childrearing is not so much the particular kinship structure as the emotional climate of the family" (p. 31). Within this context of the changing kinship structure, one of the ways that today's parents have tried to correct the imbalance created by the postmodern family is by incorporating into their family a conscientious and loving caregiver.

Caregivers serve to help parents bridge the gap between their work and family lives in helping to provide for child care as well as household management and functions. In a sense, they occupy a middle ground between the model of the modern nuclear family and its ideal image of home-centered caregiving, and the postmodern world where mothers and fathers work. Elkind describes how the old "contract" of availability of parents to their children for things like school activities and hobbies has been replaced by schedules and lists that can create a sense of pressure and anxiety in hurried children.[4] His notion of the vital family is one that fosters an interdependence in which the needs of parents and their children are balanced. It is a model that brings together the closeness and attachment of the modern nuclear family and the autonomy and independence of the postmodern permeable family.

While caregivers have always been part of upper middle class and wealthy households, they are now an integral part of thousands of dual-income and single-income families throughout the world. Where financially possible, these in-home caregivers are often the first choice for parents who must leave their children for work. Whom the parents choose as caregiver is based on a wide variety of reasons. But we have found that, in addition to the kind of person she is, the caregiver's success or failure to work for the child's (and therefore parent's) well-being hinges on the quality of the relationship between the parents and caregivers. In other words, how well they can relate to one another, navigating this new "kinship" with a monetary sum attached to it, will affect the psychological development of the child as well as the emotional climate of the entire family.

EXPANDING THE FAMILIAL SPACE—THE CULTURAL DIFFERENCES AND UNIVERSALS

Along with this expansion of the familial space to include caregivers has come the potential for broadening the family's horizons.[5] It provides both the potential for conflict and the opportunity for a rich adaptation and a greater understanding of oneself vis-à-vis others. For children, it affords the experience of input from additional sources. These adaptations can serve to expand the family's horizons in many ways—culturally, emotionally, and cognitively in terms of viewing different approaches to managing the moment-to-moment aspects of life. In particular, children get to see how their parents treat others. They see them deal with issues of communication, mutual respect, and understanding. In the face of the inevitable conflicts that arise, children see attempts at resolution, teaching them that disagreements can exist, and that interpersonal relationships can survive, evolve, and grow with them.

These opportunities and potential for conflicts and rich adaptation are heightened when caregivers come from other countries and are relatively new immigrants. However, caregivers may be acculturated, to varying degrees, just as American-born parents may be only one or two generations away from their own immigrant experience. It is particularly important for parents to be aware that their own conceptualizations of child rearing and interpersonal relationships may differ considerably from caregivers of different backgrounds. To overlook this reality can turn simple misunderstandings into potent triggers for conflict.

In her book for child care providers and educators, *Multicultural Issues in Child Care*, Janet Gonzalez Mena[6] has documented some of the core areas of potential conflict in day care settings caused by cultural differences toward basic notions of child development. Gonzalez Mena describes parents from various cultures, especially new immigrants, holding vastly different goals and ideas than educators and caregivers in our American culture. While her focus is on American caregivers and foreign parents and children, her observations apply to the reverse situation of American parents and immigrant caregivers who are acculturated to varying degrees into our typical conceptualizations of child rearing. Parents and caregivers told us that struggles can arise when it comes to these core areas that Gonzalez Mena describes.

For example, parents in other cultures may foster more dependent or interdependent relationships with children, while others may rear children for greater independence.[7] Different schedules may be emphasized for feeding and sleeping. What constitutes spoiling in one culture may be seen as comfort in another, particularly through the use of food or physical affection. Approaches to discipline and ideas about the role of adults in a child's exploration and play can also vary widely.

However, many parents described ways in which their own child-rearing approaches and conceptualizations of child development sometimes differed widely from those of other parents within their own social and economic class. Most parents would agree that providing stimulating educational toys, strictly limiting television, and engaging children directly in their play was part of their cultural ethic in the America of the 1990s. There are also variations in our culture from this ideal.

In a sense, the extended familial space is itself the creation of a new cultural entity.[8] It reflects a more global shift over the past three decades to families where both parents work. It also marks a middle point between a familial frame where mother stayed at home and father worked, and one in which both parents work and child care responsibility is shared with a non–family member. This new cultural entity contains the culture of the parents (or cultures, if they differ), the culture of the caregiver (which often can differ from each of the parents), and the individual psychologies or internal cultures of each of the members (which may differ from their own cultures as much or more than that of each of the participants). This is potentially a dizzying array of differences.

For example, what happens when an American parent who was reared generally to be independent and autonomous failed to have basic childhood needs met, such as a child in a large family? One way to resolve this conflict might be to become overly independent. This person's interpersonal stance with a caregiver, out of their conscious awareness, might sound something like this: "I don't really need anyone, and if I ever do, I will act like I don't." Imagine such a parent dealing with a caregiver from another culture. Let's say the caregiver comes from a Latino culture, for example, where, as we broadly conceive it, connections to family tend to be particularly close (what might look like dependence to us). We might expect that this same dependence would be fostered in the child-rearing approach. Suppose that this caregiver was the youngest in a large extended family, where she was often surrounded by doting family members that fostered a particularly intense version of this cultural dependence. For this parent–caregiver pair, there would undoubtedly be an intensification of conflicts. These conflicts might appear on the surface to be due simply to cultural differences, but they clearly contain the individual psychologies and unique experiences of each members. To see culture only in such broad strokes fails to capture the nuances of interpersonal exchanges. Knowing about these subtleties across cultures and the personal history that is inextricably linked to the culture is central to building and maintaining any effective relationship between a parent and caregiver. Optimally, parents and caregivers will create a blend of respect, dedication, and generosity from these intricate mutual influences. When they are blind to these influences, they work at cross purposes, and smoldering resentments form.

Among the most common examples we found of separating the culture from the individual were struggles over approaches to discipline that were attributed only to cultural differences. One mother described in broad strokes what was to her a "typical Caribbean-style rigidity" in noting the control struggles she experienced with her children's in-home caregiver. But in the same breath, this mother also seemed to have a sense that cultural generalizations often apply across cultures:

> I complain about Cora's rigidity and silence when we have a disagreement, like how to approach limiting television for Timmy (age 7). I just hate this typical blank stare I get, tinged with irritation and condescension, like she's thinking, "When he's with you and his dad, he must get whatever he feels like or else he wouldn't be hocking me about it." But you know, I can be pretty unrelenting and rigid in my own style. And it isn't always that way between me and her. Many times things run pretty smoothly and I think we collaborate pretty well in our own way.

These cultural generalizations exist for a reason. They are a short hand for attempts to organize our perceptions of others in the absence of knowing or understanding. They may be particularly helpful when we meet people from another culture either in their homeland, in our travels, or in our homeland, when they are new arrivals.

Who we are as persons, across cultures, is a complex interweaving of our inborn propensities and our earliest and subsequent experiences with our caretakers in the context of our culture.[9] To use cultural labels globally to explain interpersonal struggles may hold more than a grain of truth in some cases. Most likely, they may also represent a dynamic conflict with which we would rather not deal, a way of projecting onto others what we would prefer not to own in ourselves. Along with other psychological maneuvers, such as putting unpleasant things out of mind or casting others in the role of important persons from our own earliest experiences, this is a universal tendency.

In his book, *Beyond Culture*, Edward Hall[10] reminds us that in certain cultures it may be deemed inappropriate to speak directly about what one finds troubling. This style is counter to the way most people in our culture negotiate. For example, a caregiver's cultural propensity to talk around a request or issue bothering her and waiting for her employer to fill in the blanks may be experienced by parents in a variety of ways. The same behavior might be seen by one parent as a power struggle, by another as a manipulation, and by still another as a pull to be overly generous and nurturing, based on the dependent stance it stirs up in them. But, viewing a caregiver globally as too lax, too strict, too gratifying, or too depriving may contain more than a grain of truth. It may also contain some of the very tendencies that parents struggle with themselves.

We also heard stories from parents about differences between them that were displaced onto caregivers as cultural problems. One father, noting first that he and his wife were often at odds about his neglecting to buy enough when he went food shopping, described how the caregiver was more often blamed for the same thing during her work hours. He noted, "She's from a poor culture, it just doesn't occur to her to buy extra—even though the money is there in petty

cash." So whenever we label others, we often excuse ourselves from trying to know about them more deeply. They
can become the "other"—too different from us. Our perceptions can then easily become a self-fulfilling prophecy.

Personality styles originate in our biological needs and
capacities for learning about the world.[11] It is a universal
human experience that in our long period of dependency
from infancy to early childhood, some parental–caregiving
presence (or in some cases, more than one in extended families) provides for our needs. Caregivers from the Caribbean,
South America, Europe, and Asia, and parents from the
United States have all likely had the central human experience of some family structure (or a substitute). Struggles
around attachment to and separation from parents and
caregivers can differ across cultures, with some emphasiz-
ing greater dependence and others more independent
patterns. But these core relationships around which attachments and separations were forged come from our internal
models for relating to others.[12] This process is universal to
human development and relationships. Cross-cultural
analysis of attachment styles and separation reactions, for
example, has confirmed that individuals within cultures can
often resemble people of different cultures as much as or
more than they do people within their own cultures.[13] In
his book, *Culture and Psychology*, David Matsumoto[14] reminds us that there are many more similarities between
people of different cultures than we might imagine.

Simply put, it is important to approach others openly
with a desire to know more about their unique qualities—
their culture and their individualism, which are inextricably
linked. We relate to others based on these core experiences
that, in a sense, can transcend culture, making for valid
comparisons in understanding others. A parent's and
caregiver's individual capacities to recognize and empathize
with universal feelings about childhood and interpersonal

exchanges are much more crucial than global cultural characteristics[15] in understanding what makes or breaks the
parent–caregiver relationship. Basic struggles related to
dependency and attachment, control and autonomy, and
envy and jealousy form the bedrock of all interpersonal
relationships, whatever particular behavioral form they
take. These unconscious expectations are constantly press-
ing for expression and looking to attach themselves to situations and relationships in the present. The following
vignette is one example:

> Melissa spoke glowingly of her children's former
> caregiver, Linda, who still sent an occasional note or
> called to talk with her about how she and the children
> were doing. "It was a real shock when I discovered the
> missing money. I *had* to fire her." Melissa seemed to be
> soliciting support in the interview for her decision to fire
> Linda some three years earlier. While she couldn't re-
> call the specifics of the situation or how this theft was
> discovered, she seemed to empathize with Linda, citing
> "cultural factors." Melissa explained, "After all—she's
> from a poor South American country and had all this
> wealth and temptation to contend with" (i.e., the ready
> access to money in the house, daytime access to a com-
> fortable Manhattan apartment). "She refused to admit
> she took the $500. Like most Latinos, she must have
> been too ashamed and proud to admit she needed some
> extra money that badly. But what choice did I have—
> who else could have taken it?"

In the interview, there was a sense that the cultural and
socioeconomic explanations for this theft were a convenient
place to put feelings of betrayal and deception regarding
Linda as a person who had proven herself trustworthy over
these years. They may have represented some degree of
self-deception as well. Melissa went on to note that she

herself had come from a "dirt poor" but "proud" Southern family. She, too, "knew the value of a dollar." She described her marriage to a wealthy restaurateur that had left her "a bit scattered" when it came to money: "I tend to leave money around unattended—maybe it was too much of a temptation." We will never know if Linda had actually taken the money or if Melissa had simply misplaced it. But we can consider another possibility, given Melissa's description of this theft, her own background, and her current struggles. The situation was ripe for Melissa to psychologically *displace* onto Linda her own mixed feelings about her poor but proud background and her newfound wealth, regardless of whether Linda had taken the money. Considering this might have helped Melissa to look at some other choices.

Another caregiver, Sudha, described what was for her one of the most difficult moments in her five-year working relationship with a family with two children. She was asking for a raise and more set hours (i.e., a retainer of sorts). She initially described her reluctance as due to "cultural" differences: "I am Indian—we do not ask, we are very polite. These [the parents] are good decent people, without too much for themselves." The cultural tenets around asking directly for something she wanted presented a struggle for this caregiver. Yet when asked if she might feel the same way if she worked in a store, she became assertive, more emphatic, and direct: "Oh no! I would say it to them [the employer] if I should be paid more for my work."

Clearly, the difference here also related to the bond that she felt with this family in which she was more than an employee, an "auntie," attached to all concerned in a familial way that transcended money. Yet the money was the balance, the reality in the relationship, a felt need that had created a conflict for her in this circumstance.

CAREGIVERS IN AMERICA—FROM PAST
TO PRESENT

"From Colonial times to the present, children have lived with a bewildering variety of caretaking systems" (p. 356). In a fascinating historical survey of caregivers in American life, *Minding the Children*, Geraldine Youcha[16] wrote that women have always been enlisted to help other women with their mothering. She noted that the current cultural nostalgia for the ever-present, singularly devoted maternal figure fails to fit the reality of our historical past: "The myth of the full-time American mother as the eternal model does not fit the complex realities of the past any more than it does the practices of the present, and many of the options that exist today have had previous incarnations in only slightly different forms" (p. 13).

Throughout history, many new immigrants to this country could rely on extended family members who came with or before them to assist in the raising of their children. Others who came without built-in family supports were assisted by social supports similar to today's Head Start program or day care centers. Youcha makes the observation that even mothers who choose to stay home and care for their children, or who work as child care providers in their own homes as they likewise care for their children, are repeating an old solution practiced in this country since the beginning of the twentieth century. Indeed, the experience of the first waves of European emigration to this country was similar, as working families in the preindustrial societies melded work life and home life into their daily experience.

A wide range of social and familial supports has always existed in our culture to assist parents with child care.[16] For some parents, the extended family provided such care. For others, particularly new immigrants, early forms of day care provided the needed assistance.[17] For the upper classes, with the new wealth of the industrial society, the nanny and the mammy were a fixture of the household from the antebellum era to the present. During times of crisis, such as World War II, when women entered the work force in numbers approaching the current employment of women outside the home,[18] the necessity of child care was met with comprehensive services that would be touted today as new answers to the child care dilemma of working parents. Working mothers could rely on everything from full day child care, to afterschool care, and school vacation coverage through a cooperative web of federal, state, and local subsidies and programs.

A recent child care phenomenon, developed from the need to replace an old familial function, is another graphic example of the expansion of the familial space to include caregivers.[19] Over the past two decades, new mothers or mothers with young children have increasingly sought the help of baby nurses to assist with functions previously provided by grandmothers and aunts. This unmet need has now evolved into a new service industry of sorts—the hiring of short-term caregivers who are referred to as the "doula," which means, from the ancient Greek, the female slave. These women are lifesavers to mothers, doing everything from housekeeping and cooking to entertaining the older children and rubbing a new mom's tense back. Some hospital birthing services have even adopted the services of new agencies that specialize in these short-term all-purpose caregivers to assist with difficult labors, helping, in the view of some, to reduce the rates of cesarean section.

There is an undercurrent of negative connotations here. Some parents and caregivers speak indirectly, others more directly, about the class and status differences that exist between them as employer and employee.[20] Feelings range from an egalitarian stance of mutual understanding and

respect to outright abuse, overwork, or shirking of responsibilities, a kind of "master and slave" mentality, as more
than one caregiver and parent put it. In a small but increasingly visible number of cases, immigrants have been kept
as virtual slaves in low-paying housekeeping or child care
positions. In 1997, a New Jersey couple was held in the
brutal murder of their housekeeper and child's nanny who
had been abused over several years of "employment." [21]

A caregiver described a subtle but more common
variant of this type of control in her work as an au pair.
She was hired by a family in a relatively remote suburban-
area home where one of the parents worked out of the home
as well. Aside from difficulties that arose from time to time
with what felt like "constantly having her [the mother] over
my shoulder and in my face," this au pair felt like a
captive. "I couldn't drive and she promised me that I would
be taught at their expense so I could get out from time to
time. I never left the house for six months. I cooked,
cleaned, took care of the kids, and did all the laundry. I
think they wanted a slave because in the end when I finally gave them notice, they gave me a check and then it
bounced!"

Even those parents and caregivers who consider each
other to be a blend of extended family and employer and
employee are, to some social historians, re-creating past
abuses. It has been noted that many slaveholders in the
antebellum South described how they treated slaves "like
family." [22] Of course, most caregivers have an autonomy and
freedom to change jobs that make these comparisons less
than compelling. In addition, today both caregivers and
parents can feel "enslaved" by the difficult task of managing home and family, child care and a personal life.

Arlie Hochschild, in her book, *The Time Bind*,[23] notes
that many working parents seem to be both "prisoners and
architects" of the "time bind" by which they feel passively

enslaved. She suggests that some parents may be so stressed by the demands of postmodern family life that they may prefer the relative order, calm, and camaraderie of the office to the messy demands of child rearing. This leads to a vicious circle in which less involvement with their children and greater abdication of the parental role to the caregiver can lead to conflict, guilt, and attempts to gain control. These struggles become fertile ground for more intense and less obvious or unconscious inner struggles played out between parents and caregivers in the day-to-day care of the children.

Even these typical struggles—rivalries for the children's affections, worries about children's well-being when in the care of another, and resentments over being at the mercy of someone else's schedule—have been echoed by parents and caregivers alike in the past. More basic human dynamics seem to be the enduring source of stress and conflict in this relationship between parents and caregivers.

MOTHERHOOD IN THE 1990s: CHANGING ROLES AND EXPECTATIONS IN CHILD REARING AND THE FAMILY

In her classic book for working mothers, *Mother Care, Other Care*, psychologist Sandra Scarr[24] graphically describes the role overload and potential for excessive stress experienced by many working mothers who lead "daily lives [that] make sweatshop labor look like a vacation." It is common knowledge that working mothers of the 1990s are experiencing increasing demands as they take their place in the work force while still remaining responsible for the majority of domestic chores and child care management. It is also not surprising that difficulty in finding and maintaining a good child care arrangement can itself become a chronic stressor that impacts the psychological well-being of working

mothers.[25] Working mothers' perceived sense of control over
their child care arrangements and their ability to manage
conflicting pulls between work and family demands are
often important factors in whether these stressors become
excessive.[26]

Today's working mothers can feel spread so thin that
they may feel less sure of themselves as mothers. Here's
how Shari Thurer puts it in her book *Myths of Motherhood*: "If we enroll our children in day care, we may deprive them of personalized parental attention; if we isolate
them in the home, they may not become socialized. We
wonder if we are hurrying our children, or worse, not providing sufficient stimulation. We obsess about creativity,
values, lead poisoning, violence on television, responsible
diapers, and of course, about spending 'quality' time together. And these are only some of our concerns!" (p. xiii).[27]

Thurer's book takes a close look at the evolution of the
maternal personae from prehistory to present day, tracing
the ebb and flow of men's views of mother as selfless
nurturer to wicked stepmother and just about everything
in between. She undertook this study, in part, as a way to
cope with her personal struggle to meld together the various pulls and tugs of her own life. Her plight is indeed familiar to many working mothers who strive to maximize
both their personal potential and their role as mothers,
often struggling with guilt over these often conflicting roles.
Repeatedly during our interviewing, we found mothers and
caregivers (often themselves mothers) riddled with these
same conflicts and guilt as they grappled with efforts to
create the "perfect" caregiving arrangements.

History reveals a diversity of maternal practices and ideals that were frequently at odds. The current concept of the
ideal mother, like all ideology, is culture bound, limited to
time and place and tied to fashion.[28] Today's women at least
dare to be ambitious. But ambition and motherhood are

often seen largely as opposing forces. A willingness to put aside ambition for the sake of exclusive mothering has been looked upon by some, according to Thurer,[29] as the "virtuous proof of good mothering . . . [and] motherhood versus personal ambition represents the heart of the feminine dilemma" (p. 287). Psychoanalyst Ethel Spector Person[30] described the personal ambition–motherhood dilemma as a "curious paradox." While the working mother's absence from the home is often an economic, psychological, and personal necessity that ultimately benefits the family, women get little praise and all of the cultural blame for family stressors and child care difficulties.

Susan Chira, in her thoughtful account of the cultural debate on working mothers, *A Mother's Place*,[31] illustrates how our culture is punitive to both working mothers and their children. She notes that breaking with the old images of the good mother results in having to live with a degree of uncertainty and self-doubt. In a similar way, those mothers who choose to remain at home may feel at odds with a new ideal of the working mother as the cultural norm. Chira's conclusion is well worth quoting: " . . . the task [of motherhood] is not to find some elusive peace, but to learn how to ask the right questions to make decisions that are fair to myself and my family. I will have to constantly test the right balance between work and family, and my sense of what feels right will change over time, as my needs and my children's do" (pp. 283–284). Indeed, it is an essential task of motherhood to continually self-reflect about one's personal and familial responsibilities in order to avoid the dangers that come from using prescriptive solutions to one's unique situation.

In their comprehensive look at the family life of contemporary working parents, *She Works, He Works*, psychologist Rosalind Barnett and journalist Caryl Rivers[32] concluded that our cultural notion of the "miserable working women," hopelessly stressed, depressed, and overwhelmed, is itself a myth. They point to the fact that our cultural nostalgia for a return to the modern nuclear family at a time of insecurity and change has tuned out the many studies that show positive psychological effects and health benefits when mothers work outside the home. They also describe what they call the "collaborative couple"—a model based on their observation of the many working mothers and their partners who actively work to provide for economic security within a close family atmosphere. Their finding underscores what most working mothers know—that healthy adaptations to the challenges faced by the postmodern family *are* possible.

To the extent that all of these myths of motherhood can be understood as myths, women and men will be better able to expand on their personal options for a nurturing environment. It will give parents breathing space to create situations that correspond to what most people are already struggling with—namely, conditions where the family as a whole bears the responsibility of child care. On the national level, child rearing would no longer be seen as an individual mother's or father's problem, but where the good of all children becomes a national priority. Hillary Rodham Clinton's book, *It Takes a Village*,[33] speaks to this communal need.

The women (and men) that we listened to in formulating our ideas for this book were struggling to balance the needs of each member of the family so that no one member suffered unduly. Some were more successful than others as they navigated the rough waters of caregiving that included hiring people outside the immediate family. In most cases, those making the arrangements as well as those being hired were women. Most often, they too were working mothers, actively coping with the dilemmas of balancing work and family life.

FATHERHOOD IN THE 1990s:
MAKING ROOM FOR DADDY IN THE
EXTENDED FAMILIAL SPACE

The conflict in the changing role expectations of women in our society has its corollary for fathers as well. While the numbers of women heads of households as sole financial providers has also increased dramatically because of divorce and lifestyle decisions, so has the number of women in two-parent households who now work outside the home. We have witnessed a dramatic and unprecedented shift over the past forty years in our culture in the role of men from sole financial providers and relatively absent yet powerfully looming paternal presences to involved caregivers.[34] This shift seems to parallel a more conscious awareness of men's struggles to integrate gender and role expectations in a rapidly changing world.

James Levine,[35] a researcher and consultant on fatherhood issues, has documented the stress experienced by fathers in balancing work and family commitments. This stress was once thought to be experienced more exclusively by working mothers. Indeed, a comprehensive 1993 study of a representative sample of the American work force found no significant difference in the general levels of conflict experienced by men and women in balancing work and family commitments.[36]

Much has been written about the positive impact on the family—for children, mothers, and fathers—of the increasing role of fathers in family life, and in their children's caregiving in particular, as a result of these cultural shifts. Boys appear to benefit from a role model of the nurturing yet strong paternal presence as forged in the direct physical care and bonding with their fathers.[37] Likewise, girls benefit from a closer, nurturing contact with father.[38]

There is, however, a cultural conundrum in these positive shifts. The ideals, gender roles, and related expecta-

tions of fathers were forged in the context of more traditional maternal and paternal relationships (as is the case
for women as well). While behavioral changes, such as the
father's more direct, hands-on child care and involvement,
have become more acceptable and commonplace, underlying
identifications and internal relationships with paternal and
maternal figures or images can become a powerful source
of conflict and stress when at odds with behavior. Likewise,
in cases where economic realities are a factor in a woman's
decision to work outside the home and to opt for child care,
conflict over these decisions can also be activated for men
in terms of male identifications and ideals. The necessity
for and presence of the caregiver can therefore become a
constant reminder and potent stimulator for such conflicts.

In a number of cases it was noted that fathers who were
more directly involved with their children's care and the
caregiving relationship tended to vacillate between active
involvement and a more traditional hands-off approach. At
times they simply left the details and logistics of their
children's lives and development, from potty training to
play dates, to their wives and the children's caregiver. One
otherwise-involved father put it this way when asked about
his role in household and child care decision making: "I de-
fer to a higher authority!" Said in jest, but loaded with
meaning, he was referring to the power of the dual presence
of his wife and the caregiver of his three young children.

In the face of this dual maternal presence (mother and
caregiver), and the old cultural schema now internalized
as a way of relating and viewing himself, the father had
found an identification from childhood with his own "removed" father on the one hand and an all-encompassing
maternal presence on the other. Then, suddenly and inex-
plicably, on a conscious level (as is the nature of conflict
and feelings of ambivalence), a strong pull might be experienced to add equal time and input as an involved father

when feeling a threat from the intrusion of the caregiver or wife (as 'mother') into this new arena of male/paternal competence, autonomy, and control in the family.

One in-home caregiver captured the essence of this more traditional role that may become operative for some fathers in the face of these cultural changes. She noted: "He always seems to know what is going on, but she [the mother] deals with me directly about the day-to-day stuff. Except the money—he deals with the money. He's my boss."

Another father interviewed spoke of the difficulties inherent in having a caregiver who was older than he and his wife. He felt conflicted because, on the one hand, he wanted her to follow their lead, yet on the other he realized she was more experienced in child-rearing matters than they were. He realized that he wished the caregiver were more spontaneous in revealing things about herself, in part to make up for this age gap. He noted, "I don't think she expects to learn anything from us." Given that he and his wife were professionals with advanced degrees in their specialized fields of medicine, one can appreciate the added complications these circumstances presented.

As he reflected on the three caregivers they had employed, this father said, "You reach a point in your life when you can be manipulated by someone who is taking care of your children." He explained that he and his wife would make accommodations in order to keep things running smoothly when they felt that the person caring for their children was truly attentive, loving, and responsible. "It's a curse to have to rely on child care from people more interested in the money than they are in the care they provide." It seemed that as a physician he had an appreciation both for the need to earn a living as one who cares for others and also for what constitutes a dedicated professional versus an employee. As a father, however, there was the struggle with paternal control and the need to feel that day-to-day life was on some even, expectable keel. This can be problematic in our postmodern family structure when roles are not so neatly defined.

In a related way, the caregiver herself can sometimes come to serve a paternal function in the absence of a father figure in the family. A single mother, Mary, put it this way: "I feel she is my partner with William [her son]. I make all the decisions about him after consulting with her. Sometimes she is more attuned to his developmental needs than I am." To illustrate her point, Mary explained that William's caregiver, Tina, had felt that he was ready to go to preschool alone on the school bus. He was only 3½, and Mary felt that he might be too young, despite his enthusiasm about the idea. She noted, "I was reluctant to let him go but she explained that she would be better able to accomplish some of her other tasks at home with that free time." Mother felt that William seemed fine with the new arrangement. "She's more willing to see him making progress that I am. I guess I want to keep him a baby." In some ways, Mary was describing what is frequently seen as a paternal function that can be assumed by caregivers in their relationship to mother and child—this single mother's "partner" in a sense. Mary felt ambivalent, yet she knew that Tina was attempting to help William into the world and Tina was secure in the notion that he could manage this incremental step. Ultimately, Mary was grateful to Tina. "I'd do anything to please her and I try never to displease her by confrontations in anger. I bend over backwards." In an emotionally significant afterthought, she said, "I've already had one divorce."

3

How Parents and Caregivers Experience Their Relationship

"I can concentrate on my work knowing my child is in good hands. When I have to be in court at 9 A.M., I have to be in court at 9 A.M. No judge is interested in my story of a sitter arriving too late for work so that I'm late. Thank God I have a very responsible woman I can count on."

This is how one mother, a lawyer in private practice, described the smooth flow when everything in her life meshed as a result of the caregiver's role in the functioning of the familial space.

At the other end of the emotional spectrum, another mother described herself at the mercy of the many caregivers she had hired during the six years of her ill child's short life: "A psychological prisoner is what I am." This mother felt completely dependent on the help these caregivers provided, both physically and emotionally. Having chosen to care for her son at home, she needed all the help she could get. "I was afraid of confrontation and would adapt to their needs out of sheer desperation."

While this mother's circumstances were undoubtedly unique, her feelings were similar to those of many others we interviewed. These women ran businesses, worked in corporate settings, and managed their professional careers with success that was dependent, in real measure, on the dependability of their caregivers. For many parents, the reality of their dependency on caregivers for their day-to-

day functioning was commingled with this subjective sense
of "enslavement" to some degree. The sense of security in
leaving their children in the care of a consistently available adult, when the care is deemed "good enough," fosters
a sense of attachment and related dependency feelings for
parents, caregivers, and children, in different ways. It is
no wonder that the whole range of loving and hating feelings arise among all involved, just as it does with family.

IDEALIZING, DEVALUING, AND
THE REALITY IN BETWEEN

In many contemporary working families, caregivers provide
far more than just the day-to-day child care functions. For
many families, the presence of these caregivers not only
represents an extension of the familial space to include this
other who provides family-like functions and caregiving, but
also is an essential link within the structure of the family
itself. Frequently, we heard from parents and caregivers
alike a tendency either to idealize or, at the other extreme,
to devalue both the quality and the essential nature of the
contribution of the other.

These kinds of extreme representations may hold some
kernel of truth. We talked with caregivers who seemed
much more than "good enough" in terms of the essential
aspects of their work. At the other extreme, we heard of
and from both parents and caregivers who were marginal,
at best, or in the worst of cases, neglectful or abusive. Our
focus here is on the compelling quality of these representations that each one has of the other. When someone
speaks only in glowing or negative terms, something more
may be going on. Parents need to know what these feelings mean in their parent–caregiver relationship.

In many cases, the tendency to idealize was strongest
at the beginning of the relationship—a kind of honeymoon

period. Like most intense relationships, such as those between business partners, collaborators, intimate couples,
and the newly married, this idealization serves to cement
the attachment and to create a solid home base.[1] This reservoir of good feeling helps with negotiating the inevitable
struggles that evolve in the relationship. But this idealization by parents at the outset may also be a way to allow
themselves to leave their child with a substitute while they
are away. Struggles often arise when their hopes for the
ideal mother, perhaps the one from their own childhood
wishes, become expectations and demands of the caregiver
in the present. When these expectations clash with the
reality of the caregiver's ability to deliver, struggles arise.
Parents must understand that finding the ideal caregiver
who seamlessly provides this extended familial function is
an impossibility. Stacy Schiff[2] reminds us that even our
image of the perfectly attuned caregiver, Mary Poppins, was
a necessary fiction born of our deepest childhood wishes,
yet less ideal than we might care to know: "She can't provide references and barely manages to give a few minutes'
notice" (p. 82).

Optimally, such early idealization gradually gives way
so that parents can, if necessary, constructively criticize the
caregiver, and so that the caregiver can accept a critique
of her performance. This phase typically occurs when parents are able to adopt a more realistic and balanced view
of the parent–caregiver relationship. But parents must always be mindful that this tempering of ideals does not
mean tolerating neglect. Instead, ideals should be flexibly
maintained as a standard for parents and caregivers to
strive for in their caregiving.

Over time, especially when faced with the inevitable dis-
appointments that come, and at the end of the working
relationship, when attempting to separate from the
caregiver, a tendency to devalue or discount the caregiver

and her role may arise. For some parents, the initial idealization may never have occurred. The caregiver may remain a devalued or marginal figure—just barely good enough and always on the edge of being fired. This phenomenon was described by one caregiver placement agency owner, Joan Friedman of A Choice Nanny in New York City, as "nanny bashing."[3] Some parents, for their own deeply personal reasons, may need to hold onto the ideal or the devalued position throughout the course of the relationship. The position thus becomes a powerful self-fulfilling prophecy.

THE ESSENCE OF THE RELATIONSHIP

Dependency

We often noted these extreme views painted by both sides about the basics of the relationship—the schedule, work load, job responsibilities, and responsiveness to the children's needs. The nature of these exchanges between parents and caregivers might be described colloquially in our culture by the saying, "So what's in it for me?" This seemingly ruthless frame of reference as the basis of the relationship is something that makes the more socialized among us bristle.[4] No one likes to believe that a relationship is based on such concrete commerce. But in the earliest relationship, that between a parent or caregiver and the infant or child, in their care, this *is* the essence. This is why being a parent and caregiver can be so difficult, especially at the outset. In caregiving of infants and children, parents and caregivers purvey what is needed in a one-way arrangement. Infants and young children see us essentially in that way. We are the providers. In their world as they know it, we have everything to do with whether they have good or bad feelings. We supply what is needed, when needed (or, at times, maybe not). The person who provides is only as good (or bad) as the experience of the moment. Certainly, there are good feelings that come to the providers in this process. For example, when infants and children respond with smiles or hugs, or when we see the things they have learned from us, we are delighted. In these moments, ideally, we as caregiving adults feel given to and rewarded as well.

As much as this essential feedback keeps caregivers and parents going, we delay our rewards. We do not base our caregiving on getting them. To do so would be, in turn, treating the infant or child as if he or she were the provider, the nurturer. In this way, built into the "job description" unofficially are these needs to make oneself available to the infant and child as an "object" of provision. This is the normal, necessary developmental function of a good-enough caregiver, as we have noted. Not surprisingly, providing this function can stir up one's own feelings about wanting such needs met in these basic ways (for parents and caregivers alike). We have seen that there is often a pull for the caregiver's role in the family to be seen in this light (and for parents to be seen in this light, in turn, by caregivers).

One center child care provider described the way she experienced this in her relationship with parents:

> In the eleventh hour, when parents are picking up their child at the end of the week, you're no longer important. And that is the way it should be. You might be their life-line for as long as they need you to be, but then they want to move on and have a three-day weekend with their family. And to ask them how their weekend was when they come in, some act like, "Why are you asking me?" And if you get hurt by that, you don't understand that you are only important on Friday afternoon or the end of the work-day when you return to them a well, clean, content child. And that works well for both of you.

Many parents may forget to thank the caregiver for her work simply because it is taken for granted. This is often not the neglect of a callous employer. It is expected that care will be provided—not unlike what children come to expect when they receive good-enough care. The situation is loaded for this forgetfulness to happen. Parents must work to become aware of how the caregiver's role can often stir up such dependency feelings. Of course, there may also be more personal, individual reasons why parents may consistently disregard the caregiver and her value to the family.

Some parents and caregivers may have a tendency to treat others as useful only in terms of what they can provide, or only as good (or bad) as the last service they provided. Even under the most typical of circumstances, stressed-out parents and caregivers may forget the other's importance in this complicated relationship. Parents may be so conflicted about the role of the caregiver in the home and in the lives and hearts of their children that they protect themselves psychologically by discounting her importance. The caregiver may feel so displaced and under-valued that she presses for control with the children wherever she can. Some may even "check out" emotionally and provide only minimum custodial care. Although there are some caregivers who are unable to provide little more than custodial care regardless of their relationship with the parent, this is not our focus here. (We might wonder, however, why parents would continue to employ a caregiver who could provide only custodial care without a sense of emotional or psychological connection to the work of caring for children.)

Nurturance

For most parents, having a child stirs up dramatic feelings about one's own childhood.[5] Feelings that we all carry from our past about our relationship with our parents and early caregivers and their caregiving of us get renewed in a new and intense way when we become a parent. Our earliest needs for care, nurturance, and attachment, along with the opposing pulls for separation and autonomy, don't end abruptly with childhood. These old needs and emotional vulnerabilities accompany us as we grow and evolve in new ways, manifesting themselves in emotional reactions when caring for a child. When we observe this care being provided by someone else, either a spouse or a caregiver, the opportunity and potential for the activation of these old struggles are even more dramatic.

Intense interweavings of roles and relationships between parents, caregivers, and the children in their care can readily connect up to parents' feelings about their children as representatives of themselves from their own childhood, with all their own unresolved needs and conflicts.[6] For example, one father described the time he "caught" his children's caregiver on the phone and became overwhelmed with the vivid feeling that his children were being neglected. In retrospect, he was able to realize that in the heat of the moment he had overlooked everything else he knew about her essentially good-enough caregiving. It was only after taking time to reflect on his outsized reaction that he was able to access his own childhood feelings of neglect. He recalled a vivid memory of tugging at the phone cord as his own mother would talk for what felt like hours.

A mother became embroiled in constant struggles with her toddler's caregiver, who refused to feed him the items the mother specifically listed in a daily menu plan. As a child, this mother, the fourth of six children, was typically fed by her older (and likely resentful) siblings while her mother tended to her twin infant brothers. The feeding of her own child was now a chance to undo some terrible neglect she had experienced as a child. If the caregiver fed the child pears instead of bananas as specifically outlined, this mother would become furious and complain about the caregiver's insubordination.

The "perfect" mother, father, or caregiver is an idealized notion. It is a remnant of our own magical childhood wishes for perfect fulfillment of all our needs and reduction of any stress or unpleasure.[7] We have found that while the inclusion of the caregiver into the extended familial space is a broadening of the opportunity for good-enough care, it is also an opportunity for such complex needs and feelings to arise. Both our worst fears and our greatest hopes and ideal wishes can be played out in the day-to-day management of this relationship.

Parents and caregivers alike may, at times, turn to each other unconsciously for these needs within themselves to be provided as they observe the care of the children. A very dramatic example of this was noted around the issue of food in particular, but also around the nurturing of hopes, dreams, and personal development.

One caregiver described an ongoing struggle with a feeling of deprivation in her relationship with the mother of the children she cared for. It centered, on the surface, around her love of muffins:

> I always get myself a muffin in the morning—and when I come in and help the kids with their breakfast, I like to join them with mine. The mother gets angry sometimes, with this look like, "Can't you eat that at home on your own time?" She doesn't know I'm like, "Can't you ever buy some muffins in this house?"

This caregiver seemed to be saying that, as in most relationships, it's the little things, the little human kindnesses, that matter, that are remembered.

We also heard stories from caregivers who felt resentful about not being allowed to grow personally in terms of education or their own lifestyle. There was a sense of entitlement, often unspoken, in the subtext of these stories, that was likely born of their role in enabling the development of the children as well as the family. It is important to keep in mind that in many cultures, mothering is shared among a number of extended family members—something we can easily lose track of in our American culture where parents live apart from their siblings and their parents. Caregivers can sometimes look to their employers for a measure of the care and concern that family provides. But for caregivers, proximity to family is not the only roadblock to having these needs met, since many come from poverty. The nature of the work for the caregiver in the extended familial space can stir up powerful needs and expectations, particularly for recent immigrants in need of stability—economically, legally, and culturally. The case of Maris, a caregiver, brings these issues to life.

MARIS, AN IN-HOME CAREGIVER: "I THOUGHT I WAS WORKING FOR THE PERFECT FAMILY!"

Maris, a full-time caregiver, tearfully related her story of being fired abruptly following a series of struggles in her relationship with the mother of Sammy, now 5 years old, whom she had helped to bring up since birth. She had just received an angry phone call from Sammy's mother, telling her not to speak to her son if she should see him in the local playground where she now tended another toddler.

Maris felt shut out and abandoned herself, ostensibly in her relationship with Sammy, whom she missed terribly, but also in her long-standing relationship with his mother, Sarah. Consciously, she struggled to hold onto her idealization: "I thought I was working for the perfect family. I feel like I'm dreaming. I can't believe what happened." She described a sense of connection to Sammy, a pride in tending to his needs and in her "fit" with this family unit in which she felt like a member, not just an employee. "If I saw something on sale that they used regularly, I would just pick up an extra—like I was shopping for family." Beneath these good feelings and idealizations lurked other than positive feelings linked to real dependency binds and internal struggles for both mother and caregiver.

The disappointment and dependency conflicts went deeper for Maris, and seemed to come to a head around the time of her firing. Sarah had learned via a friend of Maris that Maris had started to take college courses at night and had became furious with her for not divulging aspects of her life that impacted on the family. Maris had been warned by other caregivers never to divulge your ambitions: "The mothers want to keep you tied down to them, not to get ahead." She spoke about her own parents' failure to give her the education she yearned for in Central America, and she vowed to do it for herself and for her adolescent son, who was living with his aunt back home.

Maris also described a paradoxical feeling of caregivers who are being legally sponsored by their employers—a deep gratitude coupled with a sense of dependency and resentment over having one's fate inextricably linked to them. Such feelings stimulated a range of reactions in Maris due to her own childhood deprivations. She angrily related her sense that she could never feel safe in complaining about her salary or about the expectations that she work additional hours without extra pay. "I'd want to say, I deserve it—it's my job, you know? Then I'd become afraid to open my mouth."

She missed her own son and felt overly attached to Sammy. "I tried not to get attached but I couldn't help it." There was a sense of intensity beyond the hoped for and expected attachment that adult caregivers and children develop. Maris's conflict was clear in her difficulty understanding Sarah's need to correct Sammy when he would call Maris "Mommy." Sarah's own difficulties were noted in the mixed messages sent to Maris about her role and her secure spot as an employee and an integral part of the family unit. Mother's Day presents came each year and many family vacations included long stretches in which Maris would tend to Sammy when his parents would be off alone. This was a particular source of pride and security for Maris. "They have family they could turn to, but they trust me best."

In this case, Sarah was struggling with sharing her son's attachment and bonding with Maris in a way that activated conflicts. She felt a need to regain control. The demand for Maris's availability to her but ostensibly for the family's scheduling needs likely represented her own needs for maternal care and attention. This dynamic was noted concretely in Maris's recollection of painstakingly and lovingly ironing Sammy's clothes. "Sometimes one of Sarah's blouses would show up on the heap and I was glad to do hers, too." It seems that the threatening call from Sarah was an attempt to express her own hurt, as if she were saying, "You can no longer attend to me, so I will use my power to deprive you of Sammy's attachment to you." Both women felt vulnerable, needy, and exploited, and they defensively took control where they could.

Thus we see that caregivers often function as the "provider" in an impossible profession—that of mother substitute or mother's helper. They not only must adapt to this expansion of the familial space, but serve, at times, to shore up the cracks from the cultural shifts that have occurred in our society over the past four decades.

Another seasoned center day care provider, Barbara, reflecting upon her twenty-five years of work, described her perspective on the caregiver's role in the family:

Blame often gets put on the caregiver. But often these couples are under a lot of pressure—financially, at work. And often, we are the place that they put it, so they complain about seeing their child in a different shirt than he wore to day care. They don't hear us say that we had to change him because of a spill. They had failed to provide a spare as requested, so we had to use one of our emergency shirts. They don't want to hear that they screwed up, that they didn't tend to it. It's their own guilt. We have rules here, and that's a reality check. It brings them back to the reality of being a parent.

Some caregivers may serve to hold together a dysfunctional family unit. One live-in caregiver, Marsha, described a chaotic household where she cared for two young girls. Mother worked part-time at home on a free-lance business, and she and her husband often traveled for business. For Marsha and the children in her care, these separations were difficult enough to manage. In addition, there was the daily routine, school schedule, and light housekeeping needed to maintain a functioning household. The most stressful part related to the mother's ongoing extramarital affair, which often left Marsha "all torn up":

I always think, "I have to protect the little ones." She [the mother] sometimes says silly things to me—"Don't come back before three," or "keep them out at the museum for as long as possible and call first before coming home." She puts it all in my face. Does she think I'm stupid? Once I did come home early. Sherry [the youngest] didn't feel so good, and I came in and saw the strange coat and it was all quiet and I knew. I just turned up the Disney tape for singing along and we went into the den. They came out later, and I knew, I could see their faces. She [the mother] was furious with me. Imagine, the nerve of her. I finally had to quit. I couldn't take it. But the kids, I still feel for them. I stayed as long as I could but I just couldn't take it. He [the father] tried to get me to stay, and I think he knew, too. He needed me, but I couldn't take it. It was too much.

It may seem that this degree of enmeshment and intensity of feeling might only or primarily occur in the case of in-home caregivers. We have seen it in other forms of child care as well. The needs being met provides for the extension of this essential familial function. These needs are universal and portable. They travel to the neighborhood family day care or day care center and are felt to one degree or another (or warded off and not felt) by all concerned.

Barbara, the seasoned center day care provider, described her sense of this overlap between care of the children and care of the parents, a familial connection that extended to her feelings about her own family:

> The parents tell me, when they have their second or third child in day care with me, "I was so silly when I worried that he [the first child] would love you more than me." It's like we're on a whole new level of relating after a few years of experience. It reminds me of when my kids started to visit as young adults after leaving home. They would bring up something I told them and say, "You know, Ma, you were right. You're pretty smart."

The daily routine either in the home, in family day care, or at the day care center puts us squarely in touch with the reality that someone else has entered our world. This other, the caregiver, is now in our inner sanctum as the familial space is extended and boundaries become permeable. We may deal with this reality in a number of ways, depending on who we are, what we bring to the situation as a parent or caregiver, and the impact that it all has on our child. Crucial to the functioning of this extended familial space is the centrality of the home base, the matrix that contains and expands this caregiving function.

THE LYNCHPIN OF THE RELATIONSHIP: ATTACHMENT, SEPARATION, AND THE INEVITABLE LOSS

As parents attempt to balance the pressures of postmodern family life and work, the demand for parenting advice has soared. A host of extremely useful books and magazines has been written by child development specialists to meet this demand for child guidance in a changing world. Contemporary authors such as T. Berry Brazelton,[8, 9] Penelope Leach,[10, 11] Selma Fraiberg,[12] David Elkind,[13] Jerome Kagan,[14] and Lawrence Balter,[15] join Benjamin Spock[16, 17] as the prominent names in this field. They all provide valuable insights for parents in conceptualizing the ages and stages of their growing child.

We have come to know much about normal developmental stages for children in terms of their physical, emotional, cognitive, and psychological milestones. However, we need to know much more, especially in terms of what constitutes a normal childhood experience in the context of the enormous societal shifts in family structures and functions that have occurred in the past few decades.[18]

Children become attached to their caregivers. They form some type of affectionate tie, a feeling of closeness, a preference that binds child and caregiver together.[19] Thus, the attachment to, separation from, and loss of this important caregiver have an impact on all of the members of this extended familial space.

The central question that seemed to run through the concerns (such as rivalry and control struggles for example) described by the parents and caregivers interviewed was, "How attached are child and caregiver to each other?" (We add, "How attached are parent and caregiver to each other?") Parents and caregivers can intuitively feel this attachment, or puzzling lack of it, both consciously and unconsciously. This attachment is a by-product of the extension of the familial space. The various conscious experiences of this attachment are a function of the parent–caregiver relationship.

Anecdotal examples from the daily lives of children, caregivers, and parents describe these feelings of attachment. Faye Dudden,[20] in her study of the history of American domestic service, found references to complex feelings of attachments between caregivers and children. Hearing a child murmur the caregiver's name in her sleep or sensing even a moment where the caregiver had usurped the mother's place in the child's affection was often a painful realization for mothers. Jonathan Gathhorne-Hardy's[21] examination of the nanny as a British institution found many similar examples. He notes that nannies would often refer to "their" children, a degree of attachment and relationship that never escaped the notice of all concerned—parents, nannies, and children. He wrote, "This acknowledgement of an ersatz relationship, which can sound rather odd to our ears, was freely admitted by 'their' children and indeed the real mothers themselves" (p. 131).

We heard stories of full-time working mothers who would count the number of hours they were with their child (including sleeping time) as a kind of emotional anchor, a concrete reminder of their more prominent role in the child's heart and mind. We also heard more balanced and adaptive measures to underscore the basic parent–child attachment, such as keeping certain intimate exchanges exclusively for themselves—nighttime baths, trips to the pediatrician, shopping for clothes, and so on. There were those parents who seemed to completely disregard the caregiver as a presence in their household. These mothers distanced themselves ("out of sight, out of mind"), particularly at times of transition or termination (see Chapter 8). Others would spontaneously mention having memories of their own childhood caregivers (typically called the "housekeeper"), or make a passing reference to keeping in touch with these caregivers, or, sadly, having attended their funerals. Children, especially when given the space to create and integrate their attachment to their caregivers, have less trouble with their feelings. One mother described her preschooler's process of experiencing and negotiating her attachment to and separation from her caregiver. After giving her caregiver a hug goodbye at the end of the day, she said spontaneously, "In the daytime I tight[en] you, and at night I loose[n] you!"

One mother reported the following dream, as she was struggling with her mixed feelings about her attachment to her children's caregiver at a time of transition. Parent and caregiver were in a planned termination process, which included the caregiver's return to college for a teaching degree, now that the children were all in school.

> I dreamt that my therapist died. In reality I stopped my sessions with her over a year ago. But in the dream I was sobbing, knowing I would miss her. But I had to deal with it and move on. I knew I had to help some schoolchildren who were in a nearby classroom—they were upset too— for she was somehow also their teacher.

This mother had talked with the caregiver just the night before about the caregiver's new work schedule, which included, in the caregiver's words, "going back into the classroom." The caregiver told the mother, "It's a little bit scary, but I'm excited. It is something I know that had to come." This caregiver and mother seemed to be experiencing, each in her own way, intense feelings about their attachment and transition, which felt like a loss and a gain for each of them. For mother, the "death" of her therapist had been of her own making in the sense that this was her dream. In the dream, she felt her own pain, but was still able to help the children on her own. Detaching herself from the image of her helping therapist while keeping her with her (the image of taking on her functions as the helper to children) was a turning point for this mother.

In a similar way, she was in the process of letting go of the connection to the caregiver, yet helping her make her transition to becoming a teacher. This mother had experienced the caregiver as a helper for the children but also as a helper for her in her career and in managing the family unit. From the caregiver's perspective, going back into the classroom was her need, her plan, but her attachment was clear. She knew such a transition and loss had to come. She felt secure with this family, but had to face this inevitable separation.

The author Jamaica Kincaid, in her novel *Lucy*,[22] presents a dream from Lucy's perspective as the nanny caring for the three daughters of Lewis and Mariah. Lucy describes how, not long after she began to work for Lewis and Mariah, Lewis had begun to refer to her as "the Visitor"—someone who seemed not a part of things and just passing through the house, as if "saying one long Hallo!," and soon would be saying a "quick goodbye!" Lewis told Lucy this one night during dinner when she thought of a dream that she felt the need to share with them:

> Lewis was chasing me around the house. I wasn't wearing any clothes. The ground on which I was running was yellow, as if it had been paved with cornmeal. Lewis was chasing me around and around the house, and though he came close he could never catch up with me. Mariah stood at the open windows saying, Catch her, catch her. Eventually I fell down the hole, at the bottom of which were some blue snakes.
>
> When Lewis finished telling his story, I told them my dream. When I finished, they both fell silent. Then they looked at me and Mariah cleared her throat, but it was obvious the way she did it that her throat did not need

clearing at all. Their two yellow heads swam toward each other and, in unison, bobbed up and down. Lewis made a clucking noise, then said, Poor poor Visitor. And Mariah said, Dr. Freud for Visitor, and I wondered why she said that, for I did not know who Dr. Freud was. Then they laughed in a soft, kind way. I had meant by telling them my dream that I had taken them in, because only people who were very important to me had ever shown up in my dreams. I did not know if they understood that.

Lewis and Mariah did know on some deeper level what Lucy meant by telling them the dream. Their discomfort about this attachment—hers and their own—was captured in their need to see her as a "visitor"—to keep a safe distance, a boundary.

One of the most historically fascinating examples of these attachments comes from the father of psychoanalysis, Sigmund Freud. In a brief reference from his correspondence with his friend and colleague Wilhelm Fliess, and in several pivotal works, the psychological significance of his nursemaid comes through.[23] With him since birth, the nursemaid was lost to him at age 2½ when she was dismissed by his parents for a household theft. In the midst of his self-analysis, he referred to his earliest caregiver in extremes of positive, negative, as well as reflective tones. On the one hand, he called her the "prime originator" of his psychological troubles. But in his reconstruction of memories from his dreams and his mother's reports, he described his sense of the nursemaid's pivotal impact on his personality and psychic life: "[She was] a woman, ugly, elderly, but clever . . . who gave me a high opinion of my own capacities." In that same letter to Fliess, he acknowledged the psychological significance that someone other than mother could have in childhood. In reflecting upon the importance of his connection or attachment to the representations of this woman for his psychological resilience he said: "If . . . I should succeed in resolving my own hysteria, I shall be grateful to the memory of the old woman who provided me at such an early age with the means for living and going on living. . . . As you can see, my old liking for her is breaking through again."

Later, in his pivotal work on dreams, he included a reference to the importance of his early attachment to his early caregiver (nursemaid) as revealed in a series of his own dreams:[24]

> Now these other dreams were based on a recollection of a nurse in whose charge I had been from some date during my earliest infancy till I was two and a half. I even retain an obscure conscious memory of her. According to what I was told not long ago by my mother, she was old and ugly, but very sharp and efficient. From what I can infer from my own dreams her treatment of me was not always excessive in its amiability and her words could be harsh if I failed to reach the required standard of cleanliness. . . . It is reasonable to suppose that the child loved the old woman who taught him these lessons, in spite of her rough treatment of him.

Pieced together from dreams, his associations to his dreams, his mother's recollections, and his burgeoning understanding of the nature of psychological development, he made a guarded, highly intellectualized reference to the impact of the loss of this caregiver. It was a pivotal point in his own early childhood in terms of separation and loss (age 2½), coupled with the absence of his mother who had just delivered his new sister: "The sudden disappearance of the nurse had not been a matter of indifference to me."[25]

These nonfamilial, yet genuine and real, attachments are perhaps a sword that cuts both ways. For the attachment to the caregiver, like the attachments to mother, can be experienced as a mixed blessing, and therefore subject to intense feelings.

The psychological and emotional significance of mother, and, in turn, the impact of her care on her developing child, has been both idealized and demonized in literature, art, religion, and psychology throughout history. Ever since Freud described the complete physical and emotional dependence of the infant on the caregiver (i.e., mother) for satisfaction and survival, there have been various attempts to describe the impact of separations and loss of this caregiving function.[26] It is now commonly understood that if chronically overwhelmed by unmet (unattended to) needs for soothing, feeding, and appropriate care, infants can feel an overwhelming form of anxiety. From our adult point of view, we might consider such early anxiety to be experienced as a fear of annihilation by overwhelming forces. Freud hypothesized that later in development, as awareness of a specific caregiving "other" developed, loss of this person providing these essential functions could stir up more intense and specific anxiety.

Considerable weight has now been given to the idea that the influence of persons and forces other than mother (e.g., father, teachers, others) have a formative impact on whom the child becomes. This happens through a process called identification. Simply put, children have a particular developmental propensity, and need to adopt as their own the ways of these important caregiving others to whom they are attached. This is accomplished through a taking in or internalization of the qualities of the earliest caregivers through increasingly more complex imitations and identifications with these important others.[27] This is a gradual process. Children are vulnerable to disruptions in the availability of these people as their capacity to adopt these caregiving and overseeing functions develops over time.

Over the years, as clinical and research emphasis has shifted to these earliest months and years of life, additional light has been shed on the nature and importance of these early attachments. D. W. Winnicott,[28] the British pediatrician and psychoanalyst, emphasized the crucial importance of an attunement to the needs of infants in these earliest months. In his view, to facilitate development, this relationship between infant and mother must be "good enough." To provide good-enough care, the mother must be realistically focused more often than not, in a well-intentioned way, on the needs of the infant over her own in order to facilitate development. Other researchers, such as psychoanalysts John Bowlby[29] and Rene Spitz,[30] described more extreme clinical examples of the impact of infants separated from mother and therefore deprived of loving handling due to institutionalization in early life. Dire consequences, such as wasting away and a failure to thrive, were noted for these infants deprived of good-enough care through this crucial lack of early attachment.

Mary Ainsworth,[31] an American psychologist and student of Bowlby, sought to explain the qualitative aspects of this attachment between children and their mothers using a psychological test she called the "strange situation." In essence, she studied the separation reactions of infants and toddlers in the first two years of life when left in an unfamiliar playroom under different stressful circumstances—when left with a stranger, or alone. She then noted their reaction when reunited with their mothers. This controlled setting was devised as a way to examine how children utilize their mothers as a safe base to return to after movements into the world. What emerged were three patterns of attachment styles: securely attached, insecurely attached with an anxious style, and insecurely attached with an avoidant style. Children described as securely attached were upset when mother left, unable to be soothed by the stranger, and then quickly calmed by a reunion with mother. Children who were described as insecurely attached and anxious were upset when left with the stranger or when left alone, but then alternately reached for, or rejected their mothers when reunited with them. Those classified as insecurely attached and avoidant seemed emotionally distant and unaffected by mother's absence and return.

Ainsworth also correlated observations of these children in the strange situation with the mothering styles observed in their homes. What she found was that children with insecurely attached styles were more likely to have mothers who were more inconsistent and emotionally unavailable in their caregiving, while mothers of securely attached children were sensitive, available, and responsive.

All of this led, predictably, to a burgeoning of research on the role of attachment in both healthy and pathological development. In the last two decades, a particular focus and concern has been the effects of nonmaternal care on infants and children of working mothers. There was an implicit message in this research—that mothers should stay at home with their children or risk dire consequences. Many of the attachment theorists that have extended Bowlby's original work and sentiment using Ainsworth's research techniques as their tool have concluded that children who must separate from their working mothers are being placed at emotional and psychological risk.[32]

Robyn Lynn Leavitt,[33] in her study of the daily life experiences of children in day care, noted that there may be an additional bias in the current literature in assuming that the attachment is (or must be) exclusively to mother. Others have concurred that crucial attachments to fathers and other important figures (such as caregivers, for example) have never been adequately examined.[34] The validity of the strange-situation test as a measure of attachment has been questioned, particularly as a way of assessing the separation and reunion behavior of children in nonmaternal care who likely show less distress simply because similar incidents occur in their daily routine. There are indications that when children in day care settings are given more time to adjust, they appear less distressed—less anxious and avoidant and more positive in their attachment styles—than brief exposures to test situations might suggest.[35]

In terms of the extended familial space, this literature might suggest that the main issue for working mothers has to do with maintaining their own exclusive attachment to the child. In turn, and by implication, this leaves out a consideration that a child may actually have some attachment to the caregiver. Developmental psychologist Carolee Howes[36] and her associates at UCLA have echoed this sentiment, noting that this expansion of the family boundaries to include caregivers provides opportunities for both "extending and challenging traditional attachment theory." Infant researcher Rudolph Schaffer[37] of Scotland's University of Strathclyde studied infants' attachments to their mothers as well as to other members of the household and came to the conclusion that innate, exclusive attachments to mother are not borne out by the research. He and his colleagues note that since infants have been found to form strong attachments to other adult relatives including siblings, there is "nothing to suggest that mothering cannot be shared by several people."

Leavitt put it this way, echoing the feelings of many child development specialists and clinicians: "Although attachment theorists may recognize that infants are capable of multiple attachments, the research demonstrating and supporting this view is rarely done, revealing a consistent bias focused on the mother."[38] Others, such as Jerome Kagan,[39] have suggested that the exclusive focus on attachment in the child–parent relationship may also overlook other important exchanges in the course of development.

A notable exception to this mother bias in attachment research is the recent work of Patricia Nachman,[40] who compared caregiver- and mother-reared toddlers in a playroom setting and at home at ages 1½ to 3. This is the height of the phase in which a separate sense of self as an autonomous person in the world is forged. This phase of separation-individuation involves a complex dance of movements away from, and returns to, home base with the person or persons to whom the child feels most attached or connected. Her researchers looked at children's emotional states, peer interests, identifications with caregiving by others as noted in their "mommy" play, and their attempts to communicate distress to their caregiver or mother. Nachman concluded what we intuitively know to be the case: "Caregivers played a very important role in the children's sense of well being and security."

There may be a variety of reasons for this bias in much of the research literature. It may be too conflictual for parents (and researchers as parents, for that matter) to consciously consider the importance of caregivers to the children in their charge. For certain mothers and caregivers, there may be a more detached style of viewing others—a kind of functional relationship as we have described where caregiving is experienced as simply a provision of supplies by another. Caregiving functions, especially early on, can understandably be experienced in this way. How one views the realities of a child's attachment to his or her caregiver may likely reveal something about the particular parent–caregiver relationship as well as what each participant brings to the relationship.

If one views this attachment as insignificant, or only a potential detractor from a crucial mother–child bond, then the separation from or loss of the caregiver is not viewed as problematic. This flies in the face of what we know intuitively—that the "loss" of this caregiving person must have some impact. Even the most well-meaning parents may underestimate their children's distress over daily separations from them as they go off to work. We believe that the same dynamic may be operative in the tendency of many parents to discount their children's attachments to their caregivers, particularly at times of separation and loss. Recognizing this attachment would mean acknowledging that they were not available to their children exclusively. We see this kind of struggle to recognize attachments in cases of divorce. Loyalty binds are common. One parent may disregard the importance of the other, especially in those understandable cases where a parent has been neglectful or, worse, abusive.

Clearly, the stability of the caregiver relationship has an impact on the quality of the ongoing care provided.[41] In turn, it impacts on the well-being of children. Research indicates that children who experience greater staff turnover in day care centers do less well in terms of preschool achievement.[42] Many parents intuitively understand the importance of the ongoing presence of and attachment to the caregiver for their children (either in their homes or in family or center day care). In a recent study of the cost of family child care, many families indicated that they would pay substantially more per week before they would seek another child care arrangement.[43] While there may be many factors involved in this decision making, certainly for many parents money is not the only consideration in evaluating the impact of the loss of their child care arrangements and particularly the impact of this loss on their child.

There are broad implications of the separation from and loss of the caregiver relationship. We know much more about the effect of separations from and the loss of important others to whom children and adults are attached. This knowledge is relevant if we consider the possibility that children do, in fact, become attached in some form to their caregivers. We make several assumptions in considering the effects of separation from and loss of the caregiver: (1) that the relationship with the caregiver does have psychological significance for children and parents, (2) that parents may deny the impact of this separation and loss for their children (and themselves), and (3) that the developmental level and degree of attachment of children is important to consider in evaluating changes in caregiving.

The Earliest Months

Because infants are dependent on others to care for them, abrupt changes in caregiving always have an effect. But in the earliest weeks and first few months of life, a good-enough response to the infant's basic needs (such as nurturance, hygiene, the rudimentary establishment of a good sleep pattern, the provision of age-appropriate stimulation, and guarding against too much stimulation) will be accepted by the infant from almost anyone who can fulfill these functions.[44] The number of hours an infant spends with a caregiver, away from mother (and father), is important to consider in evaluating the impact of an early separation. For those infants and children who spend longer days with the caregiver when mother works full time, this attachment is more likely to be a primary or central relationship, and this needs to be considered. But in these cases as well, the infant will still have the familiar others who remain to care for him. Of course, in some situations, such as when families have to relocate due to financial constraints, or when a caregiver must leave for personal reasons, parents must make caregiver changes and deal with the situation as best as possible. When it becomes clear that a caregiver is unreliable or neglectful, firing may be the only recourse. But when there may be other factors, particularly unrealistic needs, expectations, or conflicts that arise between parents and caregivers, even in these earliest months, the necessity of these separations and the loss they entail should be carefully weighed.

Moving into Toddlerhood

As development proceeds and children become increasingly attached to their caregiver, there are other crucial points where separation and loss can be even more traumatic. It is also this very attachment that can become a point of conflict between parents and caregivers. This combination of a closer bond and increased opportunity for conflicts around loyalty and jealousy, to name only a few, may lead to abrupt terminations just at the point when children are most vulnerable.

At around 6 months, the lap baby is keenly aware of the other person or persons that make up his or her world—a world where needs are met or frustrated, interests are fostered or thwarted. Moving toward the nine-month period to roughly the first year of life, we see the signs of a growing attachment to the caregiver when people who are unfamiliar (i.e., strangers) can become sources of fear and anxiety.[44] Separation and loss of a caregiver at this point may be particularly difficult to tolerate at first, because the child is now keenly aware that the new person is a stranger.

The World of the Toddler and Preschooler

When children begin to explore and separate in new ways at age 1 to 1½, they typically do so with glee and often with reckless abandon. The world is their oyster, so to speak.[45] As they feel the intoxicating power that comes with their newly acquired physical mobility, they act, at times, as if they are impervious to anything other than the immediate interest at hand. At this point, children are on the edge of an awareness that life may not always be so ideal and unrelenting in the excitement and joy that these new skills can provide. Separations at this point are therefore difficult to manage. Parents can be misled by the seeming lack of reaction to separation and loss at this point. For example, one mother described her toddler Billy's recent reaction to the loss of his full-time caregiver, Sally. Present since birth, Sally was fired for her refusal to work weekend hours. The mother told us, "Billy was oblivious to Sally's being gone. He asked about her a few times and then just did his regular routine. He seemed to like the new caregiver just fine."

Later, in the second year, with the development of speech and the tempering of this heady excitement and seeming oblivious reaction to life events, children show a more measured and a more anxious awareness that they are not so invulnerable. We see this tempering when children seek out their parents or caregivers for reassurance. While seemingly engrossed in an activity, children "check in" to make sure that this important other is still available and attentive.[45] They seek to make sure that the parents or caregivers are not displeased with them for making their own way in the world. Separations and loss at this point are more problematic. If a child could conceptualize and verbalize it, there might be an imaginary inner dialogue such as, "Why did this person leave? Did I do something to make it happen? Was my moving away into my own world connected to this loss? Is doing so a source of danger in my life?"

The way parents experience and manage the separation and loss of any sort—in this case, of the caregiver—is crucial to the well-being and ongoing development of the child at any age. Children tend to adopt their parents' style of coping with such losses.[46] Especially for older children, if parents need to disavow or devalue the loss of a caregiver and the meaning of her role in the household, it will be difficult for children to mourn her loss in their own developmentally appropriate way.

In the case of the caregiver Maris caring for Sammy (described above), there was such a rift. No one was able to acknowledge the meaning of the relationship. This appeared to lead to the termination and the particular style of handling the loss—that is, to act as if there was nothing lost, no significant event.

But what of Sammy's loss? By all accounts he was doing fine. Yet children often overtly adopt their parent's mode of dealing with crises, particularly in managing (or avoiding) feelings of loss and the necessary work of mourning. Maris noted that Sammy had been described as rebellious by several caregivers and had been overheard yelling to his most recent caregiver, "I don't have to listen to anyone but Maris." The fact that several caregivers had come and gone in only a few months is a typical phenomenon. Sammy angrily refused to attach again and again, which, for a 5-year-old, likely represented a harkening back to an earlier developmental struggle in order to cope with his loss and to avoid future losses, perhaps already anticipated. It was as if he was digging in his heels and saying, "I will take control where I can." This was his only way of coping with feeling helpless to control the dramatic (and traumatic) change in his world, unacknowledged by his parents due to their own ambivalence.

4

From Employee to Member of the Family

"It's as if she's a member of our family."

People describe this as-if relationship along a continuum. At one end of the continuum is the view that the caregiver is simply an employee. At the other end, she is viewed as a member of the family. Some days they feel one way, some days the other, with various gradations in between. Viewing the relationship in only these extremes presents a problem. By thinking of her, or the caregiver thinking of herself, in only one way or the other, both the parents and the caregiver may lose sight of the essential paradox that she is both. Parents make this flexibility possible when they expand the family boundaries to include the caregiver in this new kinship arrangement—the extended familial space. Creation of this space provides the potential for the development of strong feelings and attachments among parents, caregivers, and the children in their care. In our interviews, we found that struggles would arise when parents and caregivers failed to read each other properly, overstepping this flexible boundary, forgetting that this was an as-if relationship. The better all are able to tolerate both sides of this enigma simultaneously, the more smoothly things go.

THE DELICATE BALANCE:
NED AND MARY (PARENTS-EMPLOYERS),
NORA (CAREGIVER-EMPLOYEE)

Here is an example of what can happen when parents view the caregiver at the extremes of the continuum—only as an employee or as a member of the family. One father, Ned, described how incensed he was to see Nora, his children's caregiver of four years, waiting in the lobby of his apartment house until 7:30 A.M. before coming up to start her day:

> She was just sitting there while Mary [his wife] and I were running around trying to manage the kid's routine before we both left for work. That kind of thing makes me crazy. She knows we need her help in the morning. They're all like that. They work only when they get paid. There's no feeling.

Ned forgot that this is an as-if relationship. Nora is not a member of the family, but functions in that role in certain moments. Who could fault her for being an employee at 7:30 A.M? Mary, Ned's wife, on the other hand, seemed to forget the other side of the coin. In a separate interview, she painted the opposite picture of this caregiver. She complained about what she felt was Nora's overinvolvement with the children and her sense of propriety in the household. Nora had been very solicitous when the apartment was in need of a number of emergency repairs, which she helped to supervise. Mary remarked:

> I'd hate to have been those workmen. She was on top of them the whole time. What a perfectionist! She treated it like she was in her own home! Sometimes she forgets that she's just an employee here.

Mary lost sight of Nora's genuine concern for their well-being, something more than an employee might be expected to feel, indeed more like a member of the family. It is easy to see that the line between the participants can get blurred, especially under the pressures of daily living. Ned might have felt better toward Nora had he reminded himself that he was expecting from her what he might expect from a family member. He needed to remember that she is an employee. Mary, on the other hand, might have felt more kindly toward Nora, perhaps less threatened by her, if she could better accept Nora's desire to do her best for them while in the familial space—to go the extra mile beyond being an employee, as if she were a member of the family.

In a follow-up interview with Ned, we raised this notion. He said, "It seems like an impossible situation for all of us to be in. There are two contradictory things going on at the same time. She's my employee, yet I want her to behave, even feel, like a member of the family and pitch in the way I expect family members to do when I need them to. No wonder things get pretty messy around here at times. Sometimes it's like a juggling act."

But Ned and Mary were describing, in their own way, the paradox inherent in the relationship between parents and caregivers. Reality is one thing—Nora is an employee, they are her employers. Yet she must fit in and they must let her fit in as if she were a member of the family with all the flexibility necessary to allow for the development of strong feelings and a genuine attachment among them. This is a formidable task for all concerned. It has been our experience that conflicts of all sorts ensue where parents or caregivers forget either aspect of this paradox.

Another caregiver seemed to struggle from her perspective with similar contradictions. Chandra told about her need for respect for her time and position as well as flexibility from the parents for whom she worked in managing schedules for running the household, tending to the care of the two young boys in her charge. On one occasion, she took issue with the parents who asked her to stay late due to their own work emergency. Chandra snapped: "I had my other job to get to. I have responsibilities, too." She was referring to a part-time weekend job, which meant leaving early on Fridays, something Chandra admitted that the parents had agreed to only reluctantly. One Friday they asked her to stay an extra hour. She felt resentful, although she agreed. "I stormed out as soon as they showed up," she said.

Chandra seemed to miss the subtle reality that flexibility was a two-way street. Although she did stay that Friday night, she was furious, stuck on their having disrupted her work life, like an itinerant employee going from one job to the next. Although she admitted that the parents had tried to talk with her about working more hours for them and taking on additional responsibilities for an increase in pay, she appeared to cling angrily to the employee position, thereby retaining her distance, which, undoubtedly, was important to her. She seemed to be saying, "I want flexibility from you (i.e., be a good "family" to me) but remember, I am just an hourly employee."

WHAT'S IN A NAME?:
NANNY, AU PAIR, BABYSITTER,
CAREGIVER, DAY CARE PROVIDER

Over and over again, we discovered inevitable struggles as the family space was extended to include the caregiver. These struggles were expressed in the confusion about the label given to this other person.[1] Is she the babysitter, someone sitting in, a day mother (as several mothers succinctly characterized the relationship), a nanny, a caregiver, a special friend? What are the needs and expectations generated when the caregiver is called employee as compared to other moments in which she is referred to by one of these other labels? Shifts in which side of the paradox is holding sway at the moment express different needs and expectations that are felt by all participants. Ned's need at that moment was for all the help he could get, seeing Nora as if she were a family member. Small wonder that it is hard to describe this relationship, which is like no other, yet feels so familiar. At times the relationship between parents and caregiver, and caregiver and child overlaps other roles, defying easy or exact definitions.

Except for the European-British word *nanny* and the American word *caregiver*, there is no common word in our language that captures the complexity, emotional tone, degree of attachment, or significance of the caregiver relationship in the way that *mother* and *father*, with their obvious blood ties, connote.

The British nanny is the model for a particular blend of caregiving and boundary.[2] Not overly familiar or intimate, the nanny is connected enough to provide good care, proper example, and decorum for the upper class. The parameters of the relationship between parent and nanny are socially prescribed along the lines of servant and master, which egalitarian Americans (at least consciously) would not accept.[3] When the nanny is felt to be too attached to her charges, she may be dismissed for the seeming good of the children.[4] This action highlights the ambivalence of parents and the inherent contradiction in the relationship between the child and the nanny. Some social historians have speculated that the emotional reserve of the British middle and upper classes can be traced, in part, to the loss of early caregivers who came and went at whim.[5]

For the most part, the parents and caregivers alike in our study showed a general awareness that they wanted a healthy attachment to exist between child and caregiver. Yet the inherent struggles around the necessary expansion

of the family space to include the caregiver was often outside the conscious awareness of many with whom we spoke.
For parents to permit the caregiver to fit into the family
space, they had to consciously acknowledge that this person, who is an employee yet like a member of the family,
would inevitably put her stamp on their child. Some parents
interviewed could accept this fact, while others denied it.

The children, however, as described by parents and
caregivers, provided an important window into this struggle
to discover and label this important "other." The children
found their own unique ways to describe their relationship
to this pivotal person in their world. Even the label *nanny*,
which is defined as "nursemaid," was derived from the familiar usage in children's early language development to
refer to grandmother, that is, to another close familiar
mothering figure.[6]

You Say Donna and I Say Donny:
Klara (a Toddler) Negotiates Her Attachment
to Mother and Caregiver

One mother described her 3-year-old daughter Klara's
struggle to define her attachment to and conceptualization
of the relationship she had to her caregiver, Donna. The
child came up with a name that for her suited the situation as she experienced it.

> Klara began to call Donna "Donny" almost as soon as she
> was first able to say Donna. It was her own personal spin
> on her connection to Donna. You could hear it in her ac-
> centuation. She wouldn't simply go to gym class with
> Donna, or, in her version, with "Donny." It was more than
> that. One day she started to say, "I have class with *my*
> Donny."

It seemed that Klara's close relationship with and attachment to "Donny" was being actively constructed by all

three—mother, child, and caregiver. This mother was aware of the special relationship that Klara and Donna shared. Her pangs of jealousy coexisted side by side with a sense of relief and gratitude for the good care that Donna provided. Mother seemed able to tolerate simultaneously all of her complex feelings about this shared attachment. She was aware of and comfortable with her own ambivalence; she could therefore let Donna be Klara's "Donny," as if she were Klara's mommy at those times.

We found that, depending on their age and developmental level, children sorted out, in a nonverbal way, who's who and what's what. They do this based on the quality of the relationship that exists between the caregiver and the parents. When a parent can tolerate this relationship and allow for their own ambivalent feelings, the child stands a much better chance of finding a way to integrate these experiences in a nonconflicted way. Klara seemed to say, "No problem! This is my mommy and this is my Donny." We might imagine Klara's internal dialogue as follows: "My mommy seems to be OK with this. She knows I love my Donny. She's not mad at me for this. And she knows I love her, my mommy, too." This gradual blending and differentiation of images and feelings is not unlike the process that children go through in the course of development with their internal connections or attachments to mother and father.[7]

This child was indeed fortunate. She was not forced by a mother's insecurity to have to choose between the two. She was not made to feel a tug-of-war loyalty conflict. Rather, she was enriched by her experience of "Donny" performing mothering functions in her own personal way. This mother's healthy awareness of her mixed feelings about her daughter's special, unique attachment to "Donny" made it possible for Klara to find her own way in placing the relationship within this extended familial space. To Klara, mommy was still mommy, but there was this other, alike yet different and unique in her own right. The use of the familiar "y" ending in "Donny" (as in "mommy") undoubtedly represented a concrete connection for this child with what mothers basically do.

Gladys, a Caregiver: "She Wasn't Just a Housekeeper, She Was 'Sugar'"

Another woman described her own childhood experience with a housekeeper. While in the context of an interview about her child's caregiver, her reminiscence captured this dynamic process from her past, now alive in her present attempts to define the relationship with her child's caregiver that was like no other. Here is how she put it:

> My mother and father both worked in the family business at a time when very few women were working outside the home. They hired Gladys, a middle-aged woman from the South, to take care of the house and the kids. They called her the housekeeper. But she wasn't just a housekeeper, she was "Sugar" to us. That's what we called her, and she would call us nicknames, like "Cupcake" and "Sweetie." She was an incredible woman—patient, caring, giving of herself, always pleasant and easygoing. When my daughter was born, Gladys had retired but she was still going strong. I wanted my kids to know her, so we hired her part time. She did light housekeeping but she wasn't a housekeeper. I mean, she was "Sugar!"

It is easy to see the intense feeling and attachment this woman had for her "Sugar." Clearly, she loved her. She wanted her own children to be enriched by her, too. She wanted them to know this person who had played such a significant role in her own early life. Like Klara, she was describing a relationship to someone who is not mother yet is experienced as "like" mother. Just as Klara created the label "Donny," this woman described her attachment to her "Sugar." These labels capture the essence, the personal meaning that each associated to their attachment to their caregiver. They are the child's way of coping with the paradox that this caregiver, an employee of their parents, is at the same time experienced by them as a mother figure.

That the very young child experiences the caregiver at times as mother, not as if she were mother, adds to the difficulty inherent in the complex relationship between caregiver and parents. No wonder parents and caregivers feel at times overwhelmed in trying to navigate their feelings toward one another. It is helpful to remember that as children grow and develop, they integrate these various maternal experiences within themselves in a comfortable way, on the condition that the mother and father are not overly threatened by them. Children instinctively know what's OK and what's not OK with their parents, regardless of the verbal messages they are given.

We asked in-home caregivers how they refer to themselves. Several used the word *babysitter*. Yet when asked what they do and how they think about their work, it was clear that they felt that what they were doing was far more encompassing than the word *babysitter* captures. Frequently, their conceptualizations of their work reflected their own ideas about parental functions. It may be that the label *babysitter* (like *nanny* and *au pair*) assists many in maintaining a boundary within the relationship, a way to remember that they are "sitting in" for mother. At times, their own attachment to the child may be so compelling as to need a steady reminder.

Sudha, a Caregiver: From Nanny to Babysitter to "Auntie"

One caregiver, Sudha, at first described herself as a nanny. As she began to talk about her attachment to Michael, age 5, whom she had cared for since birth, she noted, "That does not feel right inside of me [clasping her hand to her breast].

Maybe I am a babysitter. Yes, a babysitter is better, I am
with him since he was a baby." Moments later, she corrected herself again, as she continued to talk about her feelings of attachment to the family for whom she had worked
for over five years: "In the beginning, I was just a
babysitter. Gradually, more than a babysitter I became.
Like I was in their family and feeling close to Michael, and
the new little boy. I love these kids so much."

Sudha went on to note that Michael had taken at times
to calling her "Auntie" just as her own nieces and neph-
ews referred to her on several occasions when they came
to work with her or for a playdate with Michael. It was
striking that both mother and father made a similar reference when asked how to characterize her role in their
home. While they at first used what some consider as the
more politically correct label of *caregiver*, both referred to
her as "Auntie"—a part of the family.

"She's My Babysitter, But I'm No Baby": A 7-Year-Old Describes His Connection to His Caregiver

One articulate, sensitive, 7-year-old boy, having overheard
his parents were being interviewed about their relationship
with his caregiver, described his personal feelings about the
generic label "*caregiver*": "It doesn't make any sense to me.
Who is she caring for, anyway—a 'giver'? I like *babysitter*.
It's like—she has really taken care of me since I was a
baby—she is my babysitter, you know what I mean?"

Both the unique qualities of parents and caregivers as
persons and the texture of their relationship are what make
or break the relationship. These interrelationships refuse
to be defined by simple labels or categories. They demonstrate that intense caregiving bonds exist beyond parents.
Due to her unique position within the extended family
space, the caregiver embodies a maternal quality while re-

maining her own person. Thus, it seems that there is a need for an adaptive, flexible blurring of the lines between parents and caregivers. Therefore, it is important to note that caregivers are not interchangeable (that is, in terms of firing and hiring someone) since they provide maternal and parental functions, resulting from their overlapping roles with parents.

We saw a good example of this overlapping on several occasions in the focus groups for parents to discuss the relationship between them and their caregivers. On several occasions, mothers called to ask if their children's caregiver could come to the group in their place. On the one hand, these mothers may have been thinking simply, "I can't go, so I'll send her in my place." But we might also consider a possible denial of the importance of the caregiver as a separate person (separate caregiver groups were also being held), or a less adaptive blurring of the differentiation between themselves and the caregivers, as if they were interchangeable.

We also saw many examples of more adaptive blurring of the boundaries between employee and family—within households, between caregiver functions, and among parents, children, and caregivers. Tony provided one such example. He recounted a seemingly simple but particularly meaningful experience with Tanya, his son Michael's caregiver:

> I had come home one day to help supervise the installation of some new air conditioners in the apartment. Tanya and Michael were home from the park and she was playing with him and supervising his whereabouts since the windows were open. I felt secure having her extra pair of eyes and hands, although I could have let her go home since I was there. I remember that my focus was on the workmen and she and Michael were very much in the background.

At one point, one of the workmen said that he needed a longer screwdriver to complete the job. He couldn't find one in his toolbox. Tanya spoke up: "I think we have one in the kitchen drawer." I laughed and reminded her that the one in the drawer was a tiny screwdriver we used to open Michael's scores of battery-run toys. She said, "Oh, yes, now I see, I was thinking about *my* house" (that is, the drawer in *her* house). Tanya was pitching in to help as naturally as if she were in her own home. It was only about a screwdriver (on the surface) but it had a real impact on me. I thought to myself, there is a connection to us and our home and to Michael that gets under the skin and becomes part of you.

This is an example of the adaptive blurring of boundaries. We have found that most parents call the caregiver whatever seems natural for them. However, we offer this caution: sometimes we may feel something in an emotionally compelling way and act without reflection, using our emotional conviction to substitute for rational thought. For example, one mother (unlike Klara's mother as noted above), captured how upsetting it was for her when her pre–school-age daughter would at times slip and call her caregiver "Mommy," or, in turn, would call mother by the caregiver's name: "I told the caregiver straight out—when that happens, correct her immediately!"

Who could blame this mother? Many mothers and caregivers described varying degrees of anxiety, pain, and jealousy over these slips. We might all be tempted to intervene, as this mother did, and put a stop to it because it feels frightening to think that one's child does not know who her mother is. In fact, several parents and caregivers described this very incident as a point of conflict that felt loaded symbolically for all concerned. For her part, the caregiver may fear her employer's disapproval of her, given the name the child used. One caregiver, reflecting on such an experience, spoke of her worries:

What if the child does this again, calls me "Mommy" in front of her parents? Will they be angry with me? Will they think she loves me more than them? I guess the bottom line is, Will they fire me? Sometimes I get to feeling I'm damned if I do and I'm damned if I don't. If Sally loves me, I could be fired, and if she doesn't, I could be fired. And the same with my feelings toward her. This sure is no easy job to be in!

From the parents' perspective, a mother whose child had called her by the caregiver's name said the following:

Here I am working all these hours, trying to make ends meet, to give my son the best care he can have when I'm not here—and he calls me by her name! It makes me wonder why I bother. She's going to mean more to Joe than I do. Maybe I should just stay home. Sometimes at work, I find myself envying her for the time she gets to spend with him. I think: There's something crazy about this situation.

Parents must consider a number of factors before taking action with the caregiver when something like this occurs. The reason the child is confusing the names has to do with the maternal function that both mother and caregiver perform. It does not necessarily mean, especially in very young children, that they do not know who their real mother is. They are simply saying, "Mommy and my caregiver both do mothering things for me and with me. That's why I sometimes call one by the other's name."

At less charged moments, a mother can refer to herself as "Mom" and the caregiver by name in the child's presence. This works nicely for many parents, because it allows the child, the caregiver, and the parent to observe and sort out the differences without a sense of criticism or danger.

We found in our interviews that those parents who had an understanding of their child's developmental level and worked actively to discuss moments of conflict with caregivers felt much less threatened by such incidents. Things seemed to work out more smoothly for them and between them and the caregiver. That they could speak about their feelings of envy and fear made for a more comfortable atmosphere in which no one was being blamed. Things like this happen, they felt. This helped the general feeling between them and the caregiver to remain friendly. In addition, it also helps the child develop by sorting out and learning the place each person holds with him or her in "reality."

The parent has to allow the caregiver to be experienced by the child as a "mothering other" because this is what best suits the well-being and development of the child, and ultimately the well-being of the parent. What is essential is that the mother feels that she is her child's mother. Only then will she be able to tolerate the caregiver acting as if she were the mother, yet always knowing that she is an employee.

Stephanie, a Parent, and Marcy, a Caregiver: Two Working Mothers Working It Out Together

One mother, Stephanie, took great pleasure in seeing her caregiver's love for her son, Henry. Stephanie recalled: "Marcy would have been very upset if I hadn't taken her back. Her love for Henry is so great, I know it would have devastated her if she couldn't return to care for him." Stephanie was referring to Marcy's absence following the birth of her own son, after which she had taken a short maternity leave. Stephanie never mentioned that Marcy would have been financially in crisis were she to lose her job, especially now with the added financial stress of a baby. In addition, it was significant that Stephanie never mentioned during the interview any impact of Marcy's pregnancy (for example, a shift in moods, her growing larger as delivery drew nearer). There seemed to be a need on Stephanie's part to deny the caregiver's attachment to her own new son.

Yet in another way it seemed that the way Stephanie thought about how Marcy was attached to Henry seemed to hide her own fears of losing the caregiver. She might lose this caregiver's care to the new baby. Maybe Stephanie had to focus on Marcy's love rather than her absence. It seemed to help her manage and adapt to her not being there. She could better cope with her feelings of jealousy and the worry about being left by Marcy's maternity leave. In this way, Stephanie doesn't even consider finding someone else to take care of Henry. Rather, she thinks of the situation as one in which Marcy would never leave them, so much does she love Henry. Stephanie's fears of being abandoned are tempered by an awareness of the complexity of the relationship.

Stephanie's son had been adopted, unlike the caregiver's new baby. Thus, Stephanie also had to cope with the envy she understandably had toward Marcy's capacity to bear a child. Maybe Stephanie had made her comment about Marcy's overriding love for Henry, the child in her care, as a reflection of her own internal struggles, that is, Marcy (consciously, but referring to herself, Stephanie, unconsciously) can love an adopted son as much as or more than a biological son. Also, Marcy had come to work for Stephanie only weeks after Stephanie's 6-year-old birth son had died. The caregiver had ostensibly come to help care for Henry, the newly adopted son, but she had, in essence, helped to care for this mother during a very painful mourning process as well.

Stephanie acknowledged her intense connection with Marcy. "Marcy came in, looked around, and instinctively knew what to do without my having to tell her." They hit it off immediately. Stephanie was describing a good-enough, attuned mother (for both parent and child alike, it seems).

They had good rapport, intense attachment, a reservoir of good experience, and mutual interdependence. Another employer might fire a caregiver because she lacked what Stephanie and Marcy had.

THE MANY MEANINGS OF MONEY: OFFICIAL AND UNOFFICIAL CURRENCIES

Money has a multitude of meanings. At its most concrete level, it is the means of exchange for goods and services. Yet when it comes to negotiating the salary for a caregiver's services, even more so than for other employees, much more is set in play. For example, how does one measure the worth of a person to whom you are entrusting formative functions for a beloved child?

Market value, supply and demand, and the caregiver's competence and experience determine the salary. This is reasonable. Yet we know that when it comes to money, people can be anything but reasonable. This is true for both how we amass money and how we spend it. It is a common experience of psychotherapists that patients readily discuss intimate details of their lives, including their sexual fantasies, yet they are unable or unwilling to disclose their annual income or financial worth.[8] Money is loaded!

The symbolic meanings of money play a part in the exchange between parents and caregivers.[9] Money can also be used to express a variety of interpersonal feelings and issues such as control, affection, victimization, and anger. For example, money can represent a product that one creates, and therefore a gift to a loved one. It can also represent a gift withheld from someone hated or envied. Money can be a way of setting a boundary between people. For parents and caregivers, the boundary is that between employer and employee: "You're you and I'm me, even though you may function as if you were my child's mother." Caregivers get paid, mothers do not.

For the caregiver, there is more to it than just earning a living: "I have to have it so that I don't get so involved with this child. I can never forget that this is not my child, but rather it is as if he were my child." While the need for money is real, so are the mixed feelings about having the right to ask for more, and to negotiate these rights. It can feel, to caregivers and parents alike, that they are putting a price tag on their attachment to the child. Here, too, we see the necessity of bearing the seeming contradictions of this paradox: this job is done for love *and* money. Therapists know this paradox only too well as their patients often question whether therapists can feel genuine concern for their patients' welfare while taking money for their services.

Ideally, parents never forget to give the caregiver her money, and she never forgets to take it. We say "ideally" because of the numerous "slips of mind" that we discovered. There were also subtle and not so subtle ways in which parents would count minutes and pennies due to a wide range of feelings and needs that serve to downplay the importance of the relationship. At the extreme, some parents or caregivers overextend themselves because of a range of feelings that money represents for them.

Carl, a Parent, and Melissa, a Caregiver: Money as Emotional Currency

One father, Carl, recounted that Melissa, his caregiver, seemed to decide on her own whether or not she would take a car service home instead of the subway when she stays late.

> I can't make rhyme or reason of it. I just figure when it's late and starting to get dark I want her to take the car service, because I worry about her. She has her own thing going on and sometimes she'll say no and sometimes she'll surprise me by asking for it herself.

Carl described a complex way in which both were maintaining some kind of "score" or balance between them, for their own reasons. Perhaps Melissa felt the need for this extra, concrete sign of consideration at certain moments but not at others. Perhaps feeling "considered" was sometimes enough but at other times not.

In another striking example of this interplay of reality and dynamic meanings, Carl recounted a time Melissa left for the weekend without her money.

> We were running out for the weekend and I see her envelope sitting there in its usual place on the shelf. I said, "Oh, oh, she forgot her money." I remember saying to myself should we call her or what? I just let it go. On Monday when she came in, I greeted her at the door and we said together, "The envelope," and we both laughed. Then she said, "I knew it was there, safe. It saved me from my teenagers. I just said—Don't even ask me for any more money, I don't have it!"

This vignette seemed to express an unspoken and uncanny awareness of each other's needs and boundaries—a resonance born of familiarity. Both knew the money was there and safe, meeting their symbolic needs at the moment. Carl did not phone Melissa, in part to respect her privacy and free time, and in part to give her the space to allow for the "forgetting" to be whatever it was for her. Melissa, too, had let it go in the feeling of safety that it would still be where she left it, safe for her and safe from her own difficulties with her teens' clamoring for more spending money at a time she couldn't extend herself.

People equate their personal worth with money, as if these were interchangeable. People assess how another may value them by how much they are paid for their services. Parents may feel that the salary they offer a caregiver is placing a monetary value on their child. If they allow these feelings to be enacted, they may be compelled, by feelings of guilt, to set a higher salary than they can handle. This will set up a self-defeating situation from the start. They may envy the caregiver's money due to the way she earns it. As the relationship unfolds, parents may also find themselves envying the caregiver for her chance to spend so much time with their child, something they feel they cannot do. This envy may express itself, for example, in a refusal to give a justifiable raise or to pay for overtime. Or the parents may pay the caregiver late or erratically, thereby setting up resentment in the caregiver who has her own bills to pay.

For her part, the caregiver may envy the monetary success of her employers. She might be moved to put unrealistic financial demands on them, thereby seeking to even the balance, so to speak. She may feel she has the right to help herself to whatever might be available in the household. At times, her envy may motivate her, unconsciously, to accidentally break valued, coveted objects. Reasonably, one may feel envy in all sorts of situations for all sorts of personal reasons. What is essential for the success of human interactions is that such feelings be acknowledged, through self-reflection and honesty, and then accepted as part of the fabric of the interaction. Only in this way can a person have the choice not to act in an envious way, hurtful to others, and thereby safeguard from envy's harmful potential the relationship that exists between them.

From a number of parents and caregivers, we heard the notion that their communication around money included both spoken, relatively direct, and unspoken, more indirect, exchanges. There was, in effect, an official and an unofficial salary. This very charged issue of money and its various meanings was an arena where feelings of love and money intersect.

For example, in an unofficial way, when a parent allows a caregiver to leave early, or a caregiver stays late of her own accord because the situation warrants it, or when loans or gifts are made, there is an exchange of value that goes beyond salary. This exchange is, at its core, about money or value (i.e., time is also money). On another level, these unofficial exchanges of value are more an emotional currency that speaks of understanding, attachment, dependence, caring, and generosity, about which parents and caregivers are intuitively aware. In some ways, this is not unlike the threshold function of salary in the corporate world, the way in which nonmonetary factors such as control, autonomy, flexibility, and consideration with scheduling can work to sustain employees and cement their bond to a corporation.

While we heard many stories from parents and caregivers that confirmed the separation of the relationship into its employee and the "member of the family" parts, other stories revealed a merging of these roles. For example, there were parents and caregivers who jointly shopped for certain food items, sharing good buys or special treats—everything from cereal, bagels, and challah to pot roast. Caregivers were given tickets to ballgames, new and nearly new clothing, museum memberships, and special trips and meals out with the family. Some families handed down outdated but usable computer equipment to their own children and to the children of the caregiver. Lawyers did free legal work for the caregiver and her family, doctors provided referrals to specialists, just at they would for their own family. Flexibility with the schedule, and genuine concern for the caregiver's need to be with her own family, particularly her own children at important moments such as school plays, were also part of this unofficial salary. Many parents would also provide money, ostensibly loans for things a caregiver might need but could never afford on her salary. This included airfare to visit a dying mother or father in another country, and help in paying for funeral costs.

To view these exchanges as "emotional extortion" or manipulation by parents to hold onto their caregivers, as several parents put it bluntly, overlooks the intense feelings of attachment, concern, and dependency that many parents and caregivers often feel in their relationship. The tales that many new parents hear of the best caregivers being "stolen away" by parents paying higher salaries capture the intense feelings that this relationship can engender.

Caregivers are paid hourly or salaried and work part-time or full-time based on the preferences and needs of the parents and caregiver. However, here, too, the meaning of the structure can be quite individual. In the corporate setting the difference in status and commitment between hourly and salaried workers is well known. People feel more detached when they work hourly and more attached when salaried. But in the parent–caregiver relationship, the boundaries of the payment structure, hourly or salaried, may be needed to keep one or the other aware of the paradox in the relationship, as described in Chapter 1.

The Caregiver's Lament: "Show Me the Money, But Tell Me I Have Value"

The issue of raises is particularly charged. Corporation employees can reasonably expect to have systematic reviews and annual raises. But for most of the caregivers we interviewed, there was this added dimension of the unofficial salary, the consideration of feelings, and the emotional importance and attachment as symbolized by the money. One caregiver described a common scenario:

> She [the mother] should have been generous enough to just have given me the raise. I went without one for over a year. I know they have expenses, they just had to move to a bigger apartment. But I have them, too. Prices are going up. I felt like saying, "If I didn't love your kids, I would have quit a long time ago." Why would they do this to me? Do

they want me to quit? But I don't want to have a spat
about the money. It's not just the money. In an office, they
see how you work, they have a value for you, and they
give you a raise.

When they finally offered me a raise, they said that
they would like me to do more of the cleaning since the
kids were all in school. They said they would just fire the
cleaning lady. I said, "Don't fire her. She needs her own
money, her own job. She has a family to take care of."

Not surprisingly, this struggle around money and value
was picked up by the children in the household. The oldest, age 8, whom this caregiver had helped to rear since he
was an infant, was reported to have said to her, "I'm going
to be a baseball star for the Yankees. I'm going to make a
lot of money and I'm going to give you a million dollars!"

The management of petty cash provided another example of how monetary transactions are loaded with emotional significance. We heard story after story suggesting
there was nothing "petty" in the emotional meaning of this
small supply of money for the day-to-day running of the
household. Parents differed greatly in their styles for providing these necessary funds. Some tended to be rigid and
wanted exact documentation of all expenses. Several nannies and au pairs described it this way: "Like it's my al-
lowance or something!" Other parents were more flexible,
providing a well-stocked jar with sufficient money for emer-
gencies, without rigid rules for documentation or use ("always plenty stuffed, like the fridge," another caregiver
noted). But for some, there was less availability, and, at
the extremes, a depriving quality. There seemed to be little
or no extra household money available and no obvious economic explanations for not supplying these necessary funds.
When expenses were incurred during the caregiver's daily
management of the household, she was expected to submit
receipts for reimbursement, as if in a business setting.

A caregiver, Clarissa, captured the essence of this subtle interplay of dynamic and real issues around money and value in the relationship. She described feeling unappreciated because she was underpaid by the parents of the two preschool girls she cared for (a common theme based in the reality of the dreadfully low pay of many child care providers nationwide). She described many weekends spent in the country with the family caring for the children. She noted that the mother was often erratic regarding grocery shopping. Although Clarissa often took it upon herself to buy groceries, she didn't do this in the country. On one occasion, she described arriving at the country house and the parents simply said, "We're taking the kids out to dinner and we'll see you later." Clarissa told us, "I went into the fridge—nothing but mustard! In the cupboard there was only stale food. The nerve of her!"

Clarissa harbored a grudge because of it, noted in her familiar refrain as she described her work with this family: "They just don't appreciate me." To her the situation was not surprising but clearly intolerable. She described her feelings about not being paid regularly at the end of each week, and about being asked to stay later without overtime pay or cab fare. Clarissa noted that when she was "fixing to quit," the father took her aside. He said, "I don't know what's going on with my wife and you, but here is some extra money." Clarissa continued, "He traveled a lot and she was in charge of paying my weekly salary, which she did like she did the shopping for food." For Clarissa, this father's gesture was enough to enable her to hold on since she felt attached to the children. She also felt satisfied by this degree of recognition for her work, more so than by the "official" salary, although that too was important in its own way.

We found that difficulties arise when mothers place unrealistic expectations on the caregiver, or expect her to do without basic needs, as they at times feel they have to do. The mother must have a clear idea of what she is hiring this person to do. Is she hiring the person to be a mother to her (that is, take care of her in a maternal way)? This is something that she may not recognize as an employer, but longs for nonetheless. Or the mother may not want to perform such a function for the caregiver. Such was the case with Clarissa. That mother did not want to provide her with food, a motherly function. For the vast majority of parents, these unconscious tugs to identify with their children, to be taken care of, to have the attention their children receive often go unnoticed and unspoken. Who can blame exhausted parents for wanting such help from the caregivers not only for their children but also for themselves? Yet always they must balance this need with the reality of the caregiver as an employee, remembering it is only as if she were a member of the family. This realization helps assure that the caregiver's needs are met, so that she may be willing to go the extra mile when she can.

POINTS OF CONFLICT—POINTS OF MUTUALITY

Many caregivers described their pain in having separated from their own family, including their own children, in order to come to the United States for reasons of economic necessity. Parents, in particular, mothers, described similar reasons for their own work outside the home. While some parents expressed a degree of concern about the impact of their daily separations from their children, others felt strongly that their child care arrangement was in the best interest of the children as well as their own need for personal development. Thus, parents and caregivers shared a common experience, although differing in degree and scope. At times, it appeared to be a point of conflict as well as a place for mutual understanding and empathy between them. For some caregivers, the absence of their family and children seemed to stir up more intense pulls to attach to their new "family." Others seemed to gravitate toward a more rigid boundary, a defensive distance from the children and parents for whom they worked. Such patterns were individual and related to particular caregivers and parents and their individual early experiences growing up. These common experiences underlie the various ways in which love or attachment and money or economics were interwoven in the moment-to-moment shifts that took place in their relationship.

Cari, a Live-In Caregiver: "So You Still Want Me Back?"

The ways in which emotional struggles experienced by caregivers and mothers often paralleled each other were striking in the case of one caregiver, Cari. She had gone back to the Philippines for a six-week visit in order to get her green card. At the point of her return visit, she had been away from her 16-year-old daughter for eight years, having left her with her own mother when the child was only 8. Going to the airport, Cari remembered thinking that she would be looking for a teenager, but noted to the interviewer that when she arrived she found herself looking for the little girl she had left years before. As she spoke of this scene, it was as if she were mourning a lost child, wishing she could have back those many years she missed of her child's development.

Cari became aware that she felt she was no longer the mother of that 8-year-old she had left. Her little girl was now a teenager. It dawned on her that her own mother, who had cared for her little girl, was now more her child's mother—a painful awareness for her. It was this awareness that seemed crucial in deciding what was best in this situation for everyone concerned, because now she could

bring her daughter back with her to the States. Cari intuitively recognized that she was no longer the mother in the
same way that she was when she left. It seemed that the
unspoken purpose of this trip was for each of them to
mourn their lost time.

When Cari was asked how her daughter had reacted to
their original separation, Cari noted that she had told her
daughter she would only be gone for a year, even though
she knew that it would be longer. It was her way of trying
to deal with the loss at that time in the best way she could
while holding on to the hope of reunion. When she did return, Cari felt like a stranger to her daughter. She discussed with her daughter her personal wishes about her
daughter accompanying her to the States. She recognized
that her daughter was the one who felt that her life and
future were there, in the Philippines. But Cari also sensed
that she would be unable to tend to her daughter as well
here. At this point, moving here would be disruptive to the
teen. Some of these concerns came from Cari's own sense
that this was all too much for her, Cari, to cope with now.
In the interview, Cari seemed to be in over her head emotionally at the thought of her teenager, no longer the little
girl she had left. She was unsure how to relate to her, struggling to find an optimum solution to this difficult, painful
situation.

Martha, the Employer: "Cari Was, At That Moment, Like My Little Girl"

Cari works for a family with two teenage daughters to
whom she is very attached. She has been with them for
many years. While she lost her own child, having left her
behind in the Philippines for what felt to be their mutual
well-being, she has, in a sense, a "replacement" in her attachment to these two teenage girls, as if they were her
daughters. While this is what seems to best suit her situa-

tion, often the case for women who come to this country as child care workers who have left their own children behind, it can also delay the process of mourning what they have given up or lost. For some caregivers, this can be an adaptive way to cope with their loss, but it can also become a potential point of conflict in their adoptive families for whom they work if these attachments become too real. In some ways, it helps to consciously focus on their role strictly as an employee in order to circumvent such difficulties. Yet these powerful issues around attachment and separation have a way of making their presence felt. The better able the caregivers are to hold on to both aspects of their situation—namely, that they are both an employee and like a mother to these children—the more likely they are to manage these pulls and tugs and the less likely they are to compete with the parents for the children's affections.

In a similar vein, Cari had returned from the Philippines with a present for her employer. During the interview, the employer, Martha, spoke about thanking Cari both for this present and for her consideration in having found such a good temporary replacement for herself during her trip. Martha noted that Cari seemed worried about her replacement, reminiscent of her worry about whom had replaced her in her daughter's affections. Most importantly, Martha expressed her gratitude for Cari's having taken Martha's concerns into account, a "motherly" caregiving by Cari when she was in the midst of taking this difficult trip. Cari's comment upon her return was striking; "So you still want me back?" It revealed her own struggles with her daughter, blended now with her work family. Given what she had just experienced, it was revealing that her gift for Martha was a large wooden bowl, decorated with a carving of two birds kissing.

"Cari was, at that moment, like my little girl," Martha told us. "She was bringing this special symbol of being connected to me and our family after a long trip." We can understand this as a kind of comforting object of connection between Cari's painful losses and a bridge to her life and work in the present. On yet another level, Cari could return to Martha and her teenage daughters as if they were the little girl to whom she could return and nurture in the new life she had made for herself, a life in which she needed to be loving and nurturing rather than bitter and resentful.

We believe that the essential first step toward managing conflicts is to reflect within the privacy of one's own mind upon the different layers of meaning and feeling that are inherent in the relationship. This internal self-reflection is what ultimately helps parents and caregivers to solve the concrete problems that constantly surface and often express these deeper emotional struggles that are inevitable.

In this case, Martha's capacity to be aware that they alternate at times between Martha being Cari's "mother" and Martha being Cari's "daughter" helped her let go of aggravation and resentments about being left with a replacement. This did not get in the way of their rapport. The meaning of the gift was of central importance; as Martha said, "It wasn't anything I would choose, but it was so meaningful. It came from her heart and it told us how she felt about us and how much she needed us, especially now. We found a place for it for us to admire it together, each of us (privately) for her own reason."

5

Things Aren't Always What They Seem

> The times that I loved Mariah it was because she reminded me of my mother.
>
> The times that I did not love Mariah it was because she reminded me of my mother.
>
> Jamaica Kincaid, *Lucy*[1]

Through her protagonist Lucy, a nanny, Jamaica Kincaid captures the intensity of feeling that exists in the relationship between caregivers and mothers. Lucy tells us that her employer, Mariah, the mother of the children in her charge, can, in the best and the worst of times, remind her of her own mother. Kincaid captures the subtle truth that feelings from our past relationship with our own parents or caregivers can come alive when caring for young children.

In the complicated interweaving of roles in the parent–caregiver relationship, things aren't always what they seem. Dealing with the day-to-day routine can become sticky business. Life's seemingly mundane details (what the kids wear to a play date, eat for lunch, etc.) can readily connect with ongoing difficulties in our personalities as well as related struggles from long ago. We can find ourselves caregiving in the reality-based role of parent or parental substitute just as we once were cared for, then we unwittingly change roles and experience the children we care for as the child within us. A deluge of old, unfinished business—fears, anxieties, hopes, and struggles—can flood the present moment.

WHAT ARE WE FIGHTING ABOUT?
ECHOES FROM THE PAST

This old unfinished business from our past can show itself in a number of ways in our day-to-day dealings with important people in our lives. A person in the present can come to remind us of an important person from our earliest formative experiences. This is a normal phenomenon. It is also a universal, cross-cultural experience. Psychotherapists refer to this phenomenon as transference.[2]

There is a difference between this transference phenomenon and someone simply reminding us of someone else, which is a conscious process. But transference reactions occur outside of our conscious awareness. Things can get very intense and muddled in these moments. These transference reactions make it hard to distinguish thoughts and feelings from the past from more objective, reasoned perceptions in the present. To further complicate matters, there is always a piece of reality to hang one's hat on, to use as the excuse or explanation. Someone quiet and reserved might be experienced as withholding. Someone who is more directive might be viewed as authoritarian. A monetarily prudent person might feel depriving to one person while an overly generous type might seem ostentatious and haughty to someone else.

In all close relationships, such as those between friends, lovers, parents and children, husbands and wives, coworkers, employers and employees, and parents and caregivers, these kinds of transference reactions typically occur. Each party brings his or her "old baggage" to the relationship. This creates a potential for struggles of infinite variety and intensity. These transference feelings and reactions are a kind of template, a pattern for recognizing the familiar ways of relating to others.[3] They are, in a sense, the glue of relationships. These feelings are the ties that attract, bind, and hold us together. When our past relationships have been relatively good enough—loving, attentive, nurturing, and mutually respectful of who we are and strive to be—more often than not all goes well.[4] But when our relationships from the past have been less than good enough, things get more problematic. We still end up finding aspects of these old relationships in our current ones. These old patterns or templates remain with us.

Given the nature of the relationship between parents and caregivers the situation is ripe for these kinds of intense transference reactions to develop. A constant refrain from parents and caregivers was that good times were like happy marriages or close friendships and the bad times like spats that led to breakups or divorce.

"YOU'RE MY CHILD'S CAREGIVER, YOU'RE MY MOTHER; YOU'RE MY CHILD, YOU'RE ME"

Another parent captured this transference dynamic particularly well. A real event in the present appeared to set off overly intense feelings connected to his early experience with his own early caregiver, his mother. This occurred while observing a situation related to the care of his daughter by her caregiver, Delia. Here he describes a moment when he caught Delia on the phone:

> I had talked to her a number of times about talking on the phone. This time, I came home from work early and stood outside the door because I could hear she was on the phone. It seemed to me like forever—at least 15 minutes by my watch. When I confronted her, she basically denied it, said it was a short call. I mean when somebody gets caught and says it wasn't that long, it's really upset-

ting. But I ran with it, and went through this whole thing, like, was my daughter being neglected?

And then it occurred to me, that when I grew up, I remember tugging on the phone chord, saying "Ma, Ma, Ma," when my mother would go on and on in some phone conversation oblivious to me. There were times that I would stand at the bottom of the stairs yelling to my mother who was having coffee with her mother upstairs—"Ma, Ma, Ma"—just trying to get her to notice. I know I must have felt neglected then. And I thought that my daughter was being neglected too with Delia on the phone, even though I found her happy as a clam playing with her Barbie at Delia's feet. Delia on the phone set things off. Thinking she was neglectful didn't square with everything else I knew about her and all the things she had done right.

For this father, aspects of his past had been stirred up in the present and seemed to color his perceptions. This does not mean, however, that a parent shouldn't respond to the piece of reality that was a concern and had set off a more extreme reaction. These reactions should be a kind of alarm bell—a signal to take note, to pay attention. But in this case, it started out more like a civil defense siren, wailing a signal of impending disaster instead. This kind of overkill had been triggered by the intense feelings from the past.

When this parent sorted out past and present, he was better able to realize that Delia was an attentive caregiver. This sorting-out process involved his keeping in mind all he knew about Delia as a good-enough caregiver. His intense reaction to a genuine concern in the moment had to be weighed against this backdrop. This sorting-out process cleared some of the smoke and allowed him to consider a more central issue—Delia's defensive style. Here the work of sorting out past and present had provided him with a usable signal. It helped draw his attention to an ongoing difficulty with the relationship with the caregiver that had gone underground. Her style had made it difficult to engage her directly about what was, for him, a loaded issue—the use of the phone. His vulnerability to fears of risking Delia's inattention to his daughter in the present (and from his past, to himself) had made him avoid an unpleasant moment of confrontation with her. He now could see that he had the emotional need and the right as an employer to have the caregiver respond to this request about use of the phone. "She needs to respond when I confront her, or at least discuss with me her position about it."

SORTING OUT REALITIES
AND FANTASIES

It isn't only old feelings from past relationships that can come up in the struggles in the parent–caregiver relationship. Sometimes what is being fought about on the surface is really about something else.[5] We may fight about someone forgetting to run an errand, or failing to straighten up after themselves. But our real concerns often have more to do with some other more difficult and personal anxiety or fear that gets placed (displaced) onto another handy issue.

For example, the mother of a 1-year-old cared for by a nanny told of a very upsetting argument between herself and this caregiver. While the argument was ostensibly about money, this mother seemed to be responding to an unspoken sense that the nanny was inattentive.

> I just exploded at her. I couldn't believe that she was feeling angry at me about money. She claims she worked longer hours this week than she did. I'm sure she worked the usual 45 hours, nothing more. I keep a record. I felt like, she wanted more than she deserved and I felt hostage to it, holding Sara [the 1-year-old] in my arms. The nanny screamed, I screamed, and then Sara joined in. I told her she didn't care enough about Sara right now to stay so I told her to take the day and cool off.

This mother later said that she had a gnawing sense that something was up with the nanny, something was bothering her. When the mother asked about this the next day, she noted that the nanny said, flatly, "I'm pregnant." The money was, in a sense, not the issue. In fact, in retrospect, it still remained unclear to this mother whether the caregiver had or hadn't deserved more pay for overtime that week. What was clear was the underlying feeling that had arisen between them.

Her intuition helped decipher some meaning inherent beyond the issue of money and hours. It had become an expression of feelings that were at first inexplicable and inexpressible. This mother felt that the caregiver's interests had shifted away from her daughter to her own needs. It was an accurate perception, but one that also had personal meaning and concern for her. Yet it did not arise out of some ongoing neglect of her child by the caregiver. This kind of preoccupation with oneself and one's needs is understandable, even expected, when a woman becomes pregnant. Self-centeredness regarding the money (from both the caregiver's and the mother's perspectives) reflected much more. The caregiver was, in fact, centered on her pregnancy and her own unborn child. The mother was now able to deal with more realistic concerns. There was a need for active communication with the caregiver regarding her ability (and interest) in continuing to be Sara's nanny.

BREAKING THE CODE: UNDERSTANDING
WHAT'S REALLY UP

Often underlying concerns are avoided until some event forces them to the surface. They may be expressed in code— a symbol of the problem at hand rather than a direct reference that may be more difficult and anxiety provoking for someone to confront. This seemed to be the case in the example of Lorna, a caregiver. She described her working relationship with the parents of Michelle (age 6) and Sam (age 2) at first in ideal terms. "We could discuss things about the schedule and the kids without any bad feeling or problems. The pay was fair and they showed respect for me." Following a severe lower back strain that was related to lifting Sam, a very robust toddler, Lorna called in sick for several days. "They were very understanding—even after I told them that my doctor gave me medication and bed rest for a few weeks." But Lorna became enraged and then hurt by their response when she later called and offered to pass her set of keys to the temporary babysitter. Lorna recounted that the parents told her that their was no need: "We've already changed the locks."

Lorna recalled asking if there had been some problem in the building—a break in, some lost goods, or lost keys. "They mumbled nonsense and made some lie about having 'too many keys in circulation.' I knew they meant my keys and I hung up angry. When I called them two weeks later to say I needed more time, they called me 'unreliable' and said they didn't want me back." Lorna quipped sarcastically, "I guess you don't need my keys."

Here we have a symbolic equivalent—the keys as a metaphor for control and difficulty with feelings related to safety and attachment. It is unknown but in the realm of possibility that the parents had been squelching some concerns about Lorna's caregiving and their children's safety. Everything seemed too pat in Lorna's characterization of their good relationship. In the distance and safety that her absence afforded them all, the parents seized upon the keys as the real issue.

Let's notice the complementary way in which the issue of the keys arose. Lorna thought to ask about passing the keys to the temporary sitter. They had already changed the locks, to protect their "goods" (the children). The interviewer

asked Lorna if she could imagine why they might be concerned about their "goods." She noted, in passing, that on
only one occasion had they been angry with her. "They
yelled at me like I was a bad child—no respect at all." The
incident revolved around Lorna's having "passed" the care
of Michelle to another caregiver for half an hour during gym
class while she did the grocery shopping with Sam. One can
imagine a similar scenario if one of the children's parents
were alone with the two of them and needed to run an
errand. But here, Lorna was overstepping the boundary as
employee. Despite the feeling of attachment and propriety
regarding the children, she was still sitting in for the parents.

Another way in which the past comes alive to distort or
shape the perception of the present is when our own issues
or dynamic aspects of our own personalities get displaced
onto our frustrations with others. Sorting out our part in
the situation can provide us with the information we need
to manage the ongoing relationship. Here's another example.

The way in which Michele actively struggled to find an
optimal balance between her career and tending to her son
Marc was very adaptively played out in her relationship
with his caregiver, Gracie. Michele described her own ambivalence about working while Gracie was off having "fun"
with Marc. She gave Gracie numerous free choices regarding the time she and Marc spent together. While she would
make suggestions for activities, they shared the task of
picking suitable ways for his hours away to be spent. It was
important to Michele that Gracie was happy with her working conditions. For example, while Michele had some worry
about Gracie's preference for setting up play dates with her
sitter friends in other neighborhoods (where she had previously worked), she reassured herself that it was her own
separation anxiety. She never doubted Gracie's ability to

navigate the city. She seemed to identify with Gracie's need to feel some measure of control and autonomy in her work, and as she spoke of this perspective, Michele seamlessly wove references to similar wishes in her work life.

Michele was able to keep separate (and most importantly, to privately process) her conflictual feelings regarding her relationship with Marc, whom she shared to some degree with Gracie. In our view, this was essential for her ability to help maintain a good-enough relationship with Gracie. She described this dynamic process when she recounted a moment of panic and rage she experienced one night when she was unable to find a pacifier to soothe Marc during his earliest months.

> I was frustrated and then enraged at Gracie in my mind. What had she done with his pacifier? I needed it *now*, not in the morning when I could ask her. I recall stopping in my tracks. It was as if the pacifier was for me. She tended so well to Marc and by extension to me. Right now I needed something from her and she was unavailable. In that moment I realized how much I too relied on her. My anger dissolved into a chuckle.

THE TIES THAT BIND—AND THE TIES THAT GRIND

All parties can gain enormously from a more long-term parent–caregiver relationship in terms of reliability, continuity, consistency, and attachment to the children. But parents and caregiver alike can also come to feel the price of such an attachment. The very ties that bind can become, over time, a source of interpersonal difficulty. This is often the case when these inevitable feelings, common to all intense relationships, are not processed and understood in an ongoing way. Many parents and caregivers spoke of making genuine efforts to maintain a good working relationship.

They would typically let things slide in order to avoid unpleasant or angry exchanges. This approach, however well
intentioned, often resulted in simply making nice, so to
speak. Doing so tended to bury feelings of anxiety, irritation, anger, and resentment that were themselves only the
tip of the iceberg, or the signal of distress. This is not unlike taking an aspirin for a persistent high fever without
knowing the cause. The fever just keeps coming back. Another mother put it this way:

> I didn't like it that she had her friends [other caregivers
> and children in their care] drop by without my knowing. I
> let it slide because, well, she was basically doing a good
> job and Katie loves her and is thriving. But I wondered if
> they were hanging out with each other and letting the kids
> go wild. One day, I found crackers on the carpet in Katie's
> room and we have a strict "no eating" policy in the bed-
> rooms. Finally one day I merely said, "Susie, I found crack-
> ers in the bedroom. You know there is a rule." She got
> really defensive and said one of the other kids [visitors]
> must have left it. It was like she didn't feel responsible.

This mother sounded extremely angry in the interview
as she related the story. There was a sense that she may
have delivered her simple question with an accusatory
edge. That kind of confrontation often comes with the ac-
cumulated irritation of having let important things slide.

In the case of another caregiver, Tira, even more intense,
unspoken issues between mother and caregiver, based in
their own pasts, derailed the relationship:

Tira, who refers to herself proudly as an "Irish nanny,"
has worked for two families both as a live-in and currently,
a live-out caregiver. In the interview, she focused on her
abrupt resignation from her current caregiver position following "over five years of loyal service" caring for Emily,
now in kindergarten. While the parents had their reasons
for terminating her work arrangement, Tira sensed a feel-

ing of resentment and lack of concern for her as a "real
person" by the parents, particularly the mother.

> I knew that with Emily in kindergarten, there would be
> less for me to do, but I was willing to be flexible with them.
> They asked for more housekeeping to fill my time, and I
> said yes. I don't particularly like cleaning, but I wanted to
> stay on awhile, you know, to see Emily get a good start. I
> was thinking I would like to start some classes for nurs-
> ing. You know I came to this country eight years ago with
> that in mind. So I finally brought that up with the mother
> and she pitched a holy fit. I mean, screaming and every-
> thing like a banshee. And she did it in front of Emily, who,
> thanks to me, is a smart cookie and doesn't miss a trick. I
> told her [the mother] I won't be treated that way, I won't
> be her doormat, and I gave her three weeks' notice the next
> day. She went off again, like, "How could you do this to us,
> this is just a job to you." So I said, even with a regular job
> you get educational time and benefits. I couldn't believe it.
> When I was sick with the chicken pox I got from Emily,
> she "split" the cost of my sick leave and docked me half my
> pay after the first week. The doctor said mine was the
> worst case he ever saw.

Tira was furious over what was to her a lack of sensitivity and consideration for her own needs as a loyal employee, a member of the family even. She had, after all,
helped these parents bring up Emily and, in particular, had
allowed "the Mrs." to pursue her career as a chemical en-
gineer. The complex feelings between Tira and Emily's
mother were telling in this formal label ("the Mrs.") which
seemed, at this painful ending, a reflection of condescension.

Tira described old ghosts that echoed from her past relationships with her own parents and siblings:

> My oldest brother Jimmy was the one that got the educa-
> tion handed to him in Ireland. I had to come here to give
> one to myself. Here I am only trying to better myself, and

after all I did for her [the mother] raising her child and all, you think she could think about me once in a while? All these years I have tried to be flexible and let them live their life. I could have stayed back home and cared for my little sisters and brothers and have nothing to show for myself.

Tira clearly had some unconscious hope and expectation to be more than just an employee in this family. Like a good family member, she would get her rewards—an unmet need for her from her own family of origin. Then, almost in passing at the end of the interview, she mentioned that "the Mrs." had been talking of returning to graduate school herself around this time. Her competitiveness with "the Mrs." was clear, reflecting a blend of struggles. It was as if Tira experienced mother as a sibling getting ahead at her expense. She also seemed to feel like a traditional housewife who had to stay at home while her spouse went out into the world. "It's like this back home. The women slave and care for the kids and home and the men either work (if they can) or hang around with their cronies."

Tira's frustrations are reminiscent of the early struggles for mothers who remained at home, trying to carve out a life that balanced child-rearing responsibilities and a need for personal fulfillment as well as paid professional work. The situation of another caregiver, captures the subtle way in which one's individual dynamics can become played out among caregivers, parents, and children.

Terry, a middle-aged Filipino woman, had worked for a family with three children for nearly ten years. She described her difficult and painful struggle leaving her own children in her country for nearly seven of these years when she came to the United States in order to help support them. She planned to eventually bring them here to be with her. She was very attached to the children she cared for, and referred to this numerous times in the interview. Her reference to this attachment seemed a kind of refrain as she described the emotional tugs that had pulled at her over the years to stay on with the family. This attachment also appeared to reflect some kind of replacement for her longings for her own children, thousands of miles away.

On the surface, she described a current crisis in her relationship with the parents. Her need for separate vacation weeks and a conflict over her raise were the issues that had finally led her to consider moving on:

> I planned a vacation to the Philippines for one month with my husband. I told her [the employer-mother] and she made a reference right away to how she always asked me to take my vacation when they took their vacation—that their vacation should be my vacation. For ten years I did that and the first time I take my own vacation, the mother tells me right away that she can't pay me because she will have to pay another caregiver while I am away. I did not say anything. It's not fine with me. I felt so bad. She should have been a little more considerate. Working for them for ten years and this is the first time I need my own vacation, something for myself! I can't expect she'll pay me for the whole month, but for two weeks or one week? I didn't tell her how I felt. I had just told her after two years without a raise that I needed a raise. She should have known how I would feel about the money. It's like a pattern.

Terry's recognition that a "pattern" seemed to be repeated with this employer-parent was very much to the point. Their close relationship, described in very positive terms at other moments, had a compelling emotional quality that surfaced periodically, here reaching a crisis point. Earlier signals had been overlooked. Terry spoke of their having chosen her because of her reputation with another family member. She said, "They liked Filipinos and I felt safe with them. I knew they would value me." This intense, unspoken attachment had perhaps made it difficult for Terry to ask more directly for things she felt she needed and wanted. She got so much from this initial acceptance at a time when she was vulnerable, even desperate, that she was unable to express these needs until she felt more secure, financially and emotionally. She was now ready to return to her country, and more importantly to make the shift to finding her real family again.

PART II

A GUIDE TO THE PARENT–CAREGIVER RELATIONSHIP

6

The Good-Enough Relationship

What is the "good-enough" relationship? In a general sense, it is any relationship that works for both parent and caregiver. In many ways, this isn't very different from any interpersonal relationship. We all have complementary ways of working things out in relating to others. We may find others who are like us, or others to help complete parts of ourselves. Colloquially speaking, "birds of a feather flock together" or "opposites attract." We tend to view our present experiences in old, familiar terms. We can also turn aspects of our present relationships into facsimiles of those from the past.

Here are a few of the many examples of combinations of parent and caregiver relationships we have observed:

- the hands-on, directive parent who hires a relatively passive and compliant younger caregiver;
- a young parent who hires an older, typically maternal figure to take charge and direct;
- a working mother who sees her child's caregiver as her contemporary, another working mom.

Some people have a knack for finding the wrong match— one that is less than good enough. Here, too, the unseen or unconscious goal may be to repeat an old relationship. Anyone may do this, to some degree, in an attempt to work out in the present some problem from the past. In this sense, we may have found the right match, however problematic. The key is to know enough about these old patterns and struggles so that past and present can be placed in proper perspective. In this way, the present can be lived more fully, with open eyes.

SELECTION OF CAREGIVERS: CONSCIOUS CRITERIA AND UNCONSCIOUS NEEDS

What do parents look for most in caregivers? Julia Wrigley, in *Other People's Children*,[1] found that parents generally fit into two broad categories of selection criteria for caregivers—choosing similarities or choosing differences in cultural and class background and values. But for more specific selection criteria, there are a number of important qualifications and concerns. Essentials are maturity, attunement to and awareness of children's developmental needs, consistency, reliability, and honesty. Some parents also need and expect additional household and personal assistance such as running errands or doing housekeeping. Parents whose work requires travel may need additional coverage on evenings and weekends.

What do caregivers look for in parents? Most describe a need for consistent, reliable, and equitable monetary compensation. They also seek respect and consideration for their work and their personal lives. High on the list for job satisfaction is some degree of autonomy to make choices within the general job requirements. Many caregivers expressed resentment about parents who expected that they would take on new job responsibilities, often without discussion or additional recompense, such as new housekeeping responsibilities, longer hours, new pets, new additions to the family, and moving.

The conscious criteria for selection of caregivers invariably become interwoven with unconscious needs and expectations. Personal and internal motives play a crucial role in the interviewing and hiring of a caregiver, and in the development of a working relationship between parents and caregivers.

Here is an example of such personal motives. One mother and father, who had hired a series of au pairs over the years to care for their two young sons, described their hope for and expectation of a familial connection with these caregivers: "We passed over a number of girls because they didn't seem like a good fit with our family. They were from working-class families, not on a university track. It would have been more of an employee–employer relationship. We wanted someone who was attuned to education." In our interview, there was a sense that only what was familiar could give them the feeling they hoped for in their relationship with a caregiver—a familial connection. If the caregiver was too different, it would have been too difficult psychologically to have a close connection. Here, the conscious criteria (university track, educationally attuned) seemed to capture another need—for closeness via a familial fit—that they intuitively felt could only come from sameness.

There are a number of excellent guides to finding, interviewing, and hiring in-home caregivers and home day care providers, as well as evaluating day care centers. *The Working Parents' Handbook*[2] is a particularly thoughtful and comprehensive guide to managing the typical day-to-day struggles of working parents. It offers suggestions for evaluating child care needs and presents the range of child care choices available to meet these needs. It also outlines ways to interview and evaluate potential child care providers and day care centers, as well as suggestions for dealing with difficulties in the sharing of child care responsibilities such as separation problems and control issues. Sandra Scarr's pivotal work, *Mother Care, Other Care*,[3] examines the sociocultural and psychological biases faced by mothers who work outside the home, and provides a useful guide to identifying and finding quality child care, based on the developmental needs of children and the needs of working mothers.

Several magazine articles are useful references for the new parent grappling with finding and hiring an in-home child care provider. The 1993 *New York Magazine* article, "The Great Nanny Hunt,"[4] provides a good overview of some of the important considerations in hiring child care providers as well some specific data on going pay rates and employment practices. *Working Mother Magazine* gives important information for parents to consider in the article, "In-Home Child Care: Making the Match,"[5] which covers topics such as defining job requirements, determining salary and benefits, screening candidates, and conducting an interview. In a similar vein, the books, *How to Hire a Nanny*[6] and *Hiring Home Caregivers: The Family Guide to In-Home Eldercare*[7] outline these important topics and provide models for employing nannies and caregivers. There are online websites that help parents manage their child care needs. All of these sources echo what we heard from parents (and caregivers) as important criteria for hiring and establishing the groundwork for a good working relationship.

Most of these sources cover a number of essential issues to consider. The focus, however, is on the necessary questions and issues that need to be addressed in becoming an employer (or employee). But as we have described throughout this book, parents and caregivers wear both the employer–employee and "family" hats in their day-to-day frustrations and triumphs. This fact emerges very early on when seemingly conscious working arrangements are negotiated and choices are made. We believe that there are a number of central needs and motivations for parents and caregivers alike that can come into play during the search for and match with a caregiver as well as in the ongoing relationship between parents and caregivers. Over time, these less conscious dynamics often come to play a central role in the inevitable and often ongoing struggles in the relationship. Thus, parents and caregivers select each other for a range of reasons, some conscious and others unconscious. Most are a subtle interweaving of the two.

Step One: Know Thyself—A Needs Assessment

The first step is to know as much as possible from the outset about your needs for child care, the job requirements, and your expectations. Here are some core criteria that have been described by parents:

The Core Criteria

Most parents talk of wanting a safe, secure, loving, nurturing environment, and developmental experience for their children. They also describe a need and expectation for varying degrees of household assistance directly related to the care of the children and for the general running of the household. Try in this early phase to operationalize these basic needs for yourself. For example, you might pose to yourself interview questions about these typical criteria and any others that feel important to you: Here are just a few of the more typical criteria:

Safety and Security

What type of child care coverage do I need, full time or part time? What are the daily hours? Any evenings or weekends? Will I ever need coverage overnight if I need to travel? Is it important that my caregiver know infant/child CPR?

Loving and Nurturing Environment

Do I envision a working relationship that emphasizes the employer–employee contract? Do I want to encourage a close bond between the caregiver and my child? Do I hope to develop such a bond with the caregiver?

Developmental Experience

What early enrichment experiences (e.g., songs, nursery rhymes, gross and fine motor activities, reading, exposure to play materials) do I expect the caregiver to provide? Do I anticipate that the caregiver will become involved in the day-to-day positive shaping and discipline of my child's behavior? Do I have specific techniques in mind that a caregiver must follow, or do I want a caregiver whose lead I can follow?

Household Assistance

What household tasks do I need and expect the caregiver to perform? Which tasks relate to my children specifically? Which ones involve the general household functioning? Do I want some personal assistance as well?

The Specifics

These criteria are particularly important and perhaps the hardest to pin down. This is especially true for new parents who often find it difficult to anticipate the impact of the arrival of children in stirring up old issues and in changing their lives. Their own most intimate relationship with their spouse is often shaken at the roots. Including the caregiver into the dynamic mix and sorting out their relationship to and with this new person can make this initial step even more disorienting. Here's how one mother described the importance she placed on finding a good fit between her own style and the caregiver's personality:

> It's a personality thing. You want this person to mesh within the household and family. I wanted to spend time with her, to see her interact with the kids. It was important to me that she be easygoing and not overbearing. I can be pretty direct, it's my style and I didn't want someone to take offense but to appreciate my no-nonsense style.

Here are just a few of the potential sticking points that may become relevant once the specifics around these general needs are identified.

Safety and Security

What degree of monitoring and involvement do I need and expect? Do I feel that I need to know where my caregiver and child are at every moment? What health and safety issues are particularly important to me? For example, do I feel that children should never be cared for by a smoker? Do I feel that children should never eat candy and fast food or drink soda? Do I require that preschoolers always be strapped in their strollers?

Loving and Nurturing Environment

Do I feel that a caregiver should be warm but not overly physical or intimate with my child? Do I feel that I should be able to intervene if the closeness goes over some boundary? Do I need to have the caregiver leave special activities for only me to provide? Do I expect the caregiver to follow my instructions to the letter, or do I envision broad guidelines to follow as deemed appropriate by her? Do I envision a warm, collaborative working relationship, or one that is "strictly business"?

Developmental Experience

Do I expect the caregiver to offer educational stimulation? How so? If she has not had specific training, am I prepared to offer that opportunity? Do I expect enrichment experiences to come from the caregiver alone, or do I anticipate providing outside experiences (e.g., caregiver child-enrichment classes)? Do I feel (like most parents) that physical discipline is forbidden? Do I believe in using time-outs with toddlers? Do I see an infant's gentle touching as exploration? When does it become an occasion for teaching? Do I believe that throwing food off the plate when learning to eat solids is an opportunity for learning and mastery? Is it a signal that meal time is over? Should it be an occasion to discipline? Do I believe kids should always share?

Household Assistance

Do I expect the caregiver to do my children's laundry? My own and my spouse's as well? Do I expect the caregiver to do grocery shopping? Prepare meals for the children? For me and my spouse as well? Do I expect the caregiver to do light housekeeping such as straightening up and working with the children to put toys away? Cleaning?

What Does All This Mean to You?

Certainly not everything can be anticipated or known from the beginning. Both these core and specific criteria and the parent–caregiver relationship evolve over time. Yet on another level, a private, self-reflective consideration of these specific criteria will go a long way in spotting a bad match and in anticipating the rough spots.

Think Through Your Choices and Begin to Reflect on Them

Why are these core and specific criteria so important? Would any parent (or caregiver) see them as understandable and reasonable (such as the rule that children should always be in a car seat or wear an appropriate seat belt)? What are your expectations for having these criteria followed or agreeing to follow them? What might become problematic? If this is your first child care experience, use any similar experiences that come to mind to provide some realistic and emotional input (e.g., other people's children, things you've read or observed or recall from your own baby-sitting experiences). Some of the most common underlying themes that inform our needs revolve around what it means to leave one's child with another (or to care for the child of another): feelings such as anxiety, fear, guilt, jealousy, control, autonomy, and related conflicts.

Reflect on Your Childhood Experiences

Who cared for you? How would you describe that person? What do you recall about those early times? What is your relationship with that person like now? In terms of other relationships in your life, what are your positive points? Your sticking points? What are your pet peeves or hot buttons?

Identify the Negotiable and the Nonnegotiable

As you clarify your needs, from the core to the specifics via your self-reflection on their meaning to you, what is open for negotiation and what is nonnegotiable will likely become more clear. For example, upon reflection, one parent recalled the following important trigger from the past: "I know I was left in a playpen and that seemed safe to me. I want the caregiver to use one and to work with me to pick out toys to place there, some familiar, others for new experience."

The father who became enraged and then fearful about his daughter's care when he caught her caregiver on the phone (Chapter 5) was unable, early on, to make clear his expectation about use of the phone due to his own internal struggles—his own childhood experience with his mother talking "endlessly" on the phone. The mother who felt strongly about having a no-eating rule in the bedrooms let things slide while her resentment festered (Chapter 5). Knowing why this felt so important to her might have helped her to address this need early on, rather than in a "blow up."

Another father, a single parent, described his decision, following his quick needs assessment, to send his daughter to day care rather than hire an in-home caregiver. He noted that day care was less expensive (undoubtedly true, but clearly not the only issue). In terms of his schedule and his expressed desire for the "individual attention" that he was concerned she might not receive at the day care center, an in-home caregiver might have been a better fit. With further exploration he noted that he himself had a nanny when he grew up in South Africa as a child. He felt strongly that many in-home caregivers then were often underpaid and treated like slaves by some parents. He was moved as he described his own attachment to several early caregivers, and angered in his memory that his parents treated his nannies like commodities.

Other parents embraced cultural differences both as a way of expanding their children's horizons and expressing their own social and political needs. While there is no hard data to suggest that cultural transmission actually occurs, some parents do describe a very active attempt to transmit a sense of valuing the input of the caregiver in the lives of their children and in their own expanded familial space as well.

One verbally precocious 3-year-old put it this way during one of the interviews with her parents about their relationship with her caregiver: "I am half part Jewish from Mommy and half part Spanish from Daddy and a little bit part of Jamaican spice [referring to her nanny]." This reflected in part the verbal parroting that toddlers love, and in part a clear message in the family. These parents noted that their main concern was finding a caregiver who would give their child a warm, loving start. They knew they would be sending her to a religious nursery school and were already anticipating that the student (and parent) population would be "too homogeneous." Thus they welcomed their child's identifying with her nanny.

Step Two: Making Contact—The Do's and Don'ts of Interviewing

Once you've assessed your particular needs and have developed specific criteria based on a careful assessment, turn them into specific questions for the initial interview—the *phone screening.* At this point, you might choose to place or respond to an advertisement, or go by word of mouth. You might choose to work with a caregiver agency or an au pair program for prescreened referrals. You will be fielding phone calls from potential candidates. Using a careful phone screening strategy will save you time and safeguard your privacy. It will also provide invaluable information about the potential for a good fit between parent and caregiver. For example, an initial needs assessment might look something like this:

I need someone to work 8 A.M. to 6 P.M. four days a week. I want someone to work in my home. I expect that there will be one night per week when I work late, until 7 or 8 P.M. I can afford to pay $ _ per week. I will pay for overtime hours. I want someone who doesn't smoke, who is in good heath, and I will pay for a physical exam as part of the initial job requirement. I want someone with previous experience, but someone in their late twenties or early thirties, maximum. I want someone with some early childhood courses. If I liked a candidate, I would be willing to pay for such courses as part of the job package. I can offer some autonomy in the position, but I have some basics I need; for example, I want to know my child's schedule each day and where I can find him and the caregiver. This is nonnegotiable. I want someone who is friendly and who would not only fit into our family comfortably, but also be someone with whom I'd like to have an open dialogue and ongoing relationship. I want her to be loving to my child but to keep in mind that she is helping me to maintain my connection to my child when I am at work. I know myself and I am liable to be too controlling at times due to my own background. I often felt that I was left to my own devices, lost in the crowd as the middle child. I'd like a caregiver who will be flexible and realize that my organizing the schedule, especially at first, is more a reflection of me and my past than on her. I'd also like someone who, like me, will always keep the focus on my child as the collaborative effort.

Once the needs assessment is articulated, put it into questions to pose in a phone screening. Keep notes on the responses and any questions and concerns that you have during the conversation. For example:

> "Can you work from 8 A.M. to 6 P.M. four days a week? The basic salary is $ _ per week. I will also need one late evening per week, until 8 P.M. This may change at times. I will pay overtime. How is that for you? We live in [describe general area]. Could you be here by 8 A.M? I would need to leave shortly after and don't have flexibility. What neighborhood do you live in? How would you plan to travel to work? Have you worked in child care before? Can you tell me about your work history? What did you like and dislike about these positions? Why did you leave them? What do you like about child care work? Dislike about it? What ages do you like to work with? What ages do you find of less interest?"

Listen to the candidate's responses. Is she hesitant? Does she seem defensive? Too talkative and convincing or too quiet and nonresponsive? Did you have any intuitive reactions or concerns about a response? What was your initial gut feeling about her? If it was positive, the next step is conducting a thorough personal interview. In the interview, ask all the questions you have prepared ahead of time. Often the very questions we feel we can eliminate may be an attempt to side track some intuitive feeling we have that makes us uneasy. For example, one mother described preparing a question ahead of time about the candidate's willingness to support the family's Jewish religious beliefs in part by refraining from any discussion about her own religious beliefs. During the interview, she felt that so much was right about this candidate that she didn't want to insult her by asking the question. Yet she had some gnawing anxiety about the candidate's refrain at several moments in the interview, "I'm a Christian woman." When the mother posed her question, almost as an afterthought, the candidate became irritated and shouted loudly, "I cannot refrain from singing the praise of Jesus." Needless to say, this wasn't a good fit for this mother and family.

There are a number of important considerations in the personal interview. Where should you meet the candidate? If she is a total stranger, you may feel more comfortable conducting the interview in a public place, such as a coffee shop or quiet restaurant. If the person has been prescreened by an agency or through a known third party (as can often be the case when another family relocates and their caregiver is looking for a new position), you might be comfortable interviewing her in your home.

Have your questions ready and have the candidate fill out a standard employment application that includes name, address, phone, employment history with specific information about work responsibilities and ages of children cared for, and documentation such as social security number, driver's license, and immigration status. Be sure to include a request for references and a release authorization from the candidate with her signature indicating that she is willing to have these or other people contacted (such as agencies who do formal background checks). Having this form completed in your presence will help to evaluate the candidate's written skills, comprehension, and any defensiveness or inconsistency about her work history.

Here are some general questions that are useful to ask in the personal interview:

Tell me about your employment history. Describe your specific child care experience and training. Why do you choose to do child care? What interests you about it? What are the difficult parts for you? Do you have children? What hands-on role did you play in their upbringing?

Can you tell me about your personal background—where you are from, your family, your education and immigration status? Who cared for you when you were growing up? Can you describe that person?

What do you think is most important to keep in mind when doing child care? What do you think infants and children need in terms of physical care, closeness or nurturing, stimulation and learning? What might you do on a typical day with my child?

Child care is often difficult and frustrating work. What might you do if you felt frustrated? What is your idea of discipline? Do you ever feel there are times that hitting is part of discipline? Were you hit as a child? What might you do if my child was upset and crying? Having a tantrum? What would you do if you found my child choking? (Ask other questions based on your current and anticipated needs.)

If there were a stranger at the door who claimed to have an appointment that you were unaware of, what would you do? What would you do if my child developed a high fever?

Let me describe again what the position entails. (Recount here specific job requirements and expectations.) What do you think about these responsibilities and expectations?

Describe your last (or current) position. Why did you leave (or are you leaving)?

Difficulties between people are inevitable. How did you and your last employer deal with them? Have you ever felt there were personality conflicts with your employer? How would you describe your place in the household or in the life of the family?

What are your current family and personal commitments? Current health status, including any chronic illnesses or problems? Long-term goals? May I contact the references that you have provided?

Caveats

Be sure to ask the hard questions. Asking someone if she would agree to a background check for medical, legal status, and criminal history before hiring can provide important information. You may feel that enough background information is already available, particularly if, through dependable sources, the candidate is known to you to be of good character. Background checks are essential in hiring an unsupervised child care provider. There are agencies that perform such checks on caregivers. Be sure to get a written release form from the caregiver. Checks can also be done directly through the state motor vehicle department for driving infractions, including driving while intoxicated; through the local police for criminal records; and through state social service agencies if your state keeps a registry of child neglect or abuse records.

In addition, ongoing checks should be an integral part of the early phase of employment and intermittently thereafter. Stopping in at home unexpectedly can provide important information, and scheduling outside activities for your child and the caregiver, such as classes and play dates, can bring them into contact with many helpful eyes and ears. Keeping a watchful eye for the inherent stressors of child care is not the same as hypervigilance and surveillance. When there is real suspicion of neglect, parents may opt for electronic surveillance (audio, video), which can be obtained through agencies that specialize in undetectable home surveillance. In cases where neglect or abuse is uncovered, parents typically find this a confirmation of their suspicions. You can find these investigative services in your local phone directory and through parent-networking newsletters and magazines. Check with your local authorities to determine the legality of employee surveillance.

In summary, here are some general statements that can be used to guide the phone and personal interviewing process:

Write a job description based on your needs assessment ahead of time. Don't rely on your memory, which can get caught off guard in the moment by your impressions. With a clear statement in hand, you are also more free to listen and to make use of your impressions.

Don't limit yourself to questions that require only a yes-no answer. Having a verbal account from the interviewee shows how she expresses herself, thinks, responds to stress, and whether there are points of conflict or concern and possible defensiveness about them.

Listen to the voice and abrupt shifts in emotion, and watch the body language in the interviewee. Do they feel right or not?

Look for reasons not to consider an applicant. Don't limit your options or compromise.

Be wary of someone who tries to talk you into considering her when she doesn't meet your needs assessment. Don't talk yourself into a candidate especially when feeling somehow coerced or convinced to do so, either by her or by your own rationalizations.

Don't rely on or get swept up in the glowing recommendation of another. Parents often idealize relationships that are ending in order to deal with complex feelings of loss. It is important to take special note of the absence of these overly positive references. Parents who give nothing more than verification of employment `information may be sitting on anger or fear related to a marginal or abusive caregiver. Do your own careful assessment and consideration of the fit.

Watch for possible "red flags," such as your gut reactions, gaps in employment without adequate explanation or with anxious or confused explanations, frequent moves, no phone or way to contact them.

Let the candidate know you would like to check references before inviting her back for a second interview
and before making a final decision.

Step Three: Hiring—Making the Match

In our interviews, parents reported a sense that something,
often unarticulated, made them feel that this candidate was
the right (or wrong) one. With this gut reaction, things either clicked (felt like a good fit) or "clacked" (struck a dis-
sonant chord). This is the moment when intuition or gut
level—cumulative feelings and perceptions—meets the
data—the surface answers to questions. These intuitive gut
signals are extremely useful tools when we first evaluate
others in any interpersonal situation. They are invaluable
when interviewing and hiring a caregiver. These intuitive
gut signals are really automatic thinking or "knowing without knowing why." We can, if we listen to ourselves, detect the bits of data that we actually pick up with our
senses and our powers of observation that make up these
gut signals.

Gavin DeBecker, in his book, *The Gift of Fear: Survival
Signals That Protect Us from Violence*,[8] describes the importance of using one's intuition or gut reaction in evaluating any interpersonal situation, particularly when life or
limb are at risk. Based on a lifetime of experiences, both
personal and professional, he describes a hierarchy of genuine emotional reactions that are gut signals to "take note."
These signals are familiar to us in our day-to-day lives as
fear, apprehension, suspicion, hesitation, doubt, gut feelings, hunches, nagging feelings, and persistent thoughts.
They may be accompanied by physical sensations such as
a sweaty brow, clammy palms, or a racing heart. DeBecker
makes a crucial distinction between intuition and worry:
"Unlike worry, it [intuition—gut reactions] will not waste
your time."

Recall the example of the father whose daughter's caregiver, Delia, had been caught in a lengthy phone call. This father worried that the lengthy call somehow equaled neglect. He had been worried about this over time and, due to his past history, had let things go. His immediate reaction was a signal out of control, with the volume turned up by this past history, clouding his perceptions. In contrast, recall the example of the mother who instinctively knew that her argument with her caregiver over money was about a concern that the caregiver was less attentive to her child care responsibilities than usual. This mother pursued her perception to find that the caregiver was indeed preoccupied due to an acute situation—her own pregnancy (Chapter 5).

The kinds of gut feelings of which DeBecker writes are based in immediate perceptions. People feel something in their gut with clear conviction and then typically attempt to deny what they intuitively know. Such signals are pushed away. On the other hand, worries are more typically embraced, elaborated, and blown up to bigger than life proportions. This was the case with Delia, who this father worried was globally neglectful, which didn't fit the picture, as compared to this mother's intuition that the fight with the caregiver was about much more that money.

The Ones that Click

"You can't pick your mother, but you can pick your child's caregiver." While this parent's reflection rings true enough on the surface, you can still end up dealing with aspects of your relationship with your mother and your past! These old familiar connections to our past are the glue that holds relationships together.

Here's how Cynthia, a single mother, described what clicked for her when she first met her daughter's caregivers, a couple who have lived in for five years:

I had talked to several women—one who had a husband and children in Turkey, another said she would live in and then return to her family on weekends. It just depressed the hell out of me to hear these stories. Then, this couple called and asked if I would consider having them both. I said I was actually looking to make a "family" for my daughter. I was alone and needed to travel for work and didn't ever want to worry about having someone consistently there. They are Asian, and I have an affinity for Asian people. My house is very Asian. They walked in and I know I was thinking, and they must have been thinking, "This is going to work." They were charming people. He was gregarious and she was so nice. They were both teachers over there.

This couple needed a place to live and I needed to have a family support system. So they needed me as much as I needed them. And they needed to be treated like people and not servants, and I know they sensed that that would be the case from day one.

To me it's karma. I am so lucky that these people came into my life. We were always moving when I was a kid and my family was always trying to put a positive spin on it. But because of that experience I knew I wanted some stability. I was able to have a child on my own, but with their help I've been able to raise her. I obviously was looking to create a family.

In the following example, we see how a good click at the beginning, good data and intuition combined, is inevitably informed by unconscious dynamics. These dynamics influenced the form and shape of the collaboration. They also sustained the relationship to the end.

Ella knew consciously that she was looking for someone to provide for her children something she felt lacking in her own childhood—a sense of warmth and enthusiasm with which she herself struggled to connect. She described a series of difficult starts with several caregivers after the birth of her first child, Evan. "One was great and left after several months when her own teenager in Trinidad became ill. The next two came and went so quickly that I can't recall them, except that they were well recommended."

While she couldn't articulate why she fired these caregivers, she mentioned in passing, with an air of thinly veiled irritation, that these caregivers preferred to work the care of Evan into their routine rather than focus on his needs. An inconsistent nap schedule was of particular concern. Her first impression of her current caregiver of eight years, Monica, was telling: "I was looking for stability. She had grown kids and had lived in the same apartment for twenty years. She was animated, but maybe a bit too bossy. I didn't like her personally, but thought, 'This is what Evan needs.'" The click for her was not so much her feeling about the relationship with the caregiver, but a particular aspect of the relationship—her sense of what she needed for her children. She felt secure that this particular caregiver could provide this for her.

Ella's description of her own primary caregiver (her mother) seemed to reflect her less conscious sense of what she didn't get, yet intuitively grasped was important for her own children (including a second child, Lucy). Regarding her mother she noted, "I liked her." This seemed counter to her immediate response to Monica (i.e., "I didn't like her"). She described her mother as an interesting and vibrant woman, noting in passing (and seemingly without conscious awareness) her own longing for emotional contact that was missing in her internal representation of mother. There were conscious traces of ambivalent feelings about mother: "She would drag me around to 'interesting' places like her bridge club, the golf course, and, lectures on art and interior design." In a telling moment, Ella laughed and said, "I guess I was an itinerant napper."

While differences in child-rearing approaches, such as discipline style, were an ongoing bone of contention between Ella and Monica, the very aspects of Monica's personality and stability that had attracted Ella (both consciously and unconsciously) had developed into what appeared to be an ongoing struggle. Monica worked long hours. Her work involved handling major aspects of the weekday care of the children. Ella described her as controlling and, at times, possessive of the children, who were clearly very attached to her. Ella seemed keenly aware of this dilemma: "I wanted someone to love my kids. I guess I got what I wanted."

A series of events seemed on the surface to trigger a crisis in the relationship, and brought an end to their formal relationship. At this point in the interview, Ella echoed an often-heard refrain that speaks to the intensity of these emotional relationships: "It was like getting a divorce. Maybe we can be better friends after it's over." Increasingly, Monica felt unappreciated. She would accuse Ella of jealousy regarding her relationship with the children. Ella noted how absurd this idea was to her. "I wanted them to love her." It seemed that while Monica was ascribing her own issue to Ella, there was a thread of truth to this explanation. While Ella felt secure in her own relationship with her children, there was the echo of her own childhood yearnings, as in her recounting of a moment she witnessed between Monica, Evan, and Lucy.

"I came home late one night, and found them laughing and eating popcorn—all curled up together on the couch as Monica was reading them a silly rhyme book." At this moment, Ella's emotion seemed to capture a complex interweaving of regard for Monica, love for her children, and a longing for the kind of attention that they elicited and Monica was happy to provide, which was something Ella had missed when she was a child.

The breakup came at the time when Ella was more consciously aware that the children had gotten what they needed. She had every intention of continuing the connection on some informal level for the children (and herself, it seemed). Now Ella's own adult needs and wishes could be more central. "Monica and I were at odds about how to manage the household now that the children were older. She was good at running a child-centered place. Now that they are in school, I'd like things to be different." She noted intuitively, "I need my own space in my own home." Thus, there was a facilitative quality to this relationship, which had now outlived its purpose and was no longer needed in the same fashion. This shift is not unlike the passing of certain parental functions onto children who internalize these functions as development forges on.

The Ones that Clack

One parent described, in retrospect, a moment of realization when hiring a caregiver. In the initial interview, she recalled being taken in by the caregiver's charming style and Louisiana accent, something she had always enjoyed. The caregiver came well recommended through a friend of a friend. That gave the parent a sense of security. The candidate was very chatty and had lots to offer, presenting her résumé, including experience in a day care center, about which she talked glowingly. But this mother remembers that while there was a feeling of clicking with this woman, taken in closely and feeling close, there was also a gnawing feeling, a distant clack that didn't quite sit right. She noted:

Whenever I asked her to do something, every response was the same; "Alright then. Okay then. Splendid. Splendid." She was too agreeable. She did everything I asked, but I felt uneasy and shrugged it off. The next day, I was a little bit taken aback when I opened the door and saw the new caregiver's face shift abruptly from a scowl to that same friendly cast and chirping style. I shrugged it off again. Everything seemed fine when we spent several hours together. She and my 3-year-old daughter were happily playing with her blocks when at that point, according to plan, I left for a few hours to attend a business meeting.

During the meeting, mother received a frantic phone call from the caregiver, reacting as if she had already been blamed for something, the 3-year-old screaming in the background. The mother recalled:

I half expected a call, I mean it was my daughter's first day with the caregiver. But there was something else gnawing at me. I kept thinking about and then pushing away that scowl. I came home right away. I was still thinking mostly that this is expected, this is a new caregiver, my daughter hadn't spent much time with her. Then, I began to think, what if my daughter is sensing this scowl, too?

After she settled her daughter down for a nap, mother decided to talk things out with the new caregiver.

I said, matter of factly, to the caregiver, "This is new for all of us—my daughter, me, you. And you can imagine how it must be for me, leaving my daughter with somebody new. I just would feel better if I could talk with you more about your work at the day care, like how did they deal with separation problems and so on." And then I saw it again, the caregiver's friendly chirping voice and smile turned dramatically. She scowled at me, and hurled at me in a threatening voice: "Don't you trust me? Am I not doing a good job?"

In that moment I knew that the gnawing feeling was something I couldn't overlook. I mobilized myself. I called work and said I wouldn't be back for the rest of the day. I called my backup in the apartment building for the rest of the week. And then I told the caregiver, "I appreciate your watching my child for two days. I will pay you for the week. But I don't feel we can work well together." It was as if she didn't hear me. She began to negotiate, to explain, to pour on the charm. I just repeated myself and she left. I was never so relieved in my life when she walked out the door.

Another mother described the initial clack she experienced with a caregiver in the first interview. This gut feeling had been pushed away at first and she hired the caregiver. Over the course of several weeks, it became more clear to her that not only was this caregiver a bad fit for her and for the family, but that the caregiver appeared to have more extreme personality problems than she had first imagined.

She seemed great in the first interview. Very pleasant, self-assured. She had day care training and experience with other families and knew a lot about child development. She had a car, which was important since my kids have to be driven to the park and school and various activities. But when I asked her what she liked about child care, why she did it, she had this funny reaction. Her whole demeanor changed. She seemed really pissed and snapped back at me: "Of course I like my work, I'm a child care provider." It felt creepy to me but I brushed it off. I mean, I didn't want to offend her at this point. I just figured that maybe she was feeling I had belittled her with the question—like she was "just" a child care worker.

The father, who had a variable work schedule, also attempted to make things work despite his reservations:

Part of me knew it wasn't working out. I know my wife had asked her to do certain things and she hadn't followed through. But on the off chance that something could be worked out, I tried to talk to her. I told her that if things were going to work out, she had to listen to my wife, what she expected in terms of the daily plans and schedule. I told her that she essentially ran her company as the operating vice president but that a day or two a week she would be working out of the house. I said she should think of this as an employer–employee relationship. It's like you're her assistant. After I finished talking she stared at me—like a deer caught in headlights at night—for what seemed like minutes. It was like a petit mal seizure. And then she said flatly, "OK." I had this weird feeling after.

Mother described a series of struggles over the next weeks around control of the schedule that ultimately led to her firm decision to fire this caregiver. For a few days it seemed that the caregiver had heard what her husband had said. The caregiver seemed to be a little more pleasant, agreeing to the daily plans and schedule. It was at this point that the mother began to have *second doubts* about her decision to fire the caregiver. This was a slip of the tongue from the familiar expression, *second thoughts*. Again this mother had felt intuitively, a *second doubt*, a gut feeling that this was not working, that the fit was far from good enough.

The final straw was that the caregiver arrived a half hour late to pick up the child at nursery school. Mother noted: "I had made it explicit, how important it was that she be picked up on time." This was a concrete example that could be relied on, even though in the initial interview the clack was a perception of another sort.

She told the caregiver of her decision to terminate her employment at the end of the sixth week.

She was very calm at first and asked me the reason. I just told her the fit didn't seem right. Then she turned and screamed at me in a repetitive chant, "She warned me about you. She warned me about you." She was referring to the last caregiver who had left amicably after four years with us to return to school full time. We had a good ongoing relationship since she left. This felt so out of left field and crazy to me. Then she calmly discussed the morning routine with this pleasant smile as if nothing had just happened. I said to myself, Who is this person? To go from a rage to this other place? Then I knew I had made the right decision, just six weeks delayed.

TAKING THE GIANT STEP

There is a good fit between your caregiver candidate and your family's needs, and you've taken the next step and hired her to care for your children. Now the hard part begins! The caregivers (in fact, anyone in a new employment situation or relationship) are typically on good behavior, and the parents are watchful during this trial period. But there are ways of evaluating and being watchful without becoming a judge or detective. Working with someone to fine-tune the job responsibilities and requirements in a collaborative mode is not the same as making demands and taking control.

Practical Arrangements

Dealing with the core contractual aspects of the caregiver's employment, such as schedule, pay and raises, vacation time, sick leave and personal days, and work responsibilities, is crucial to the caregiver arrangement. What the parent expects and what the caregiver is willing to do is important to address up front. Basic child care responsibilities and any other expectations must be spelled out precisely. To do otherwise is to court crises and struggles around both the care of the children and the running of the household. Communication is central to negotiating these contractual aspects of the job.

The Dry Run: Setting the Tone in the Early Days

The first days after hiring should be a gradual orientation for the caregiver to your child, your household, and the nuances of the job requirements. This is the period when the tone is set for the working relationship that parents and caregivers can expect over the course of their collaboration. It may also be the period when it becomes more clear that an initially good match—a click—may in fact be a clack. Here are some suggestions for this early period:

- Show the caregiver the child's typical routine. Ask for her thoughts and input and try to find areas of agreement.
- Review the current job expectations and schedule.
- Show her where she can keep her personal belongings.
- Ask for input regarding any supplies or toys that she feels would be useful to have available.
- Point out areas of your home that you want to be private (from her and guests).
- Review safety procedures and provide all necessary emergency numbers.
- Review any nonnegotiable issues in terms of the work expectations.
- Let her know, in a good-natured way, about any special needs or pet peeves of yours and other family members. Ask about any of hers as well.
- Collaborate on a written log to keep track of the daily events, schedule, and milestones for your child.
- Set up a regular time to discuss the days events and a weekly time for status reports.

Getting Started

In his book, *The Orphaned Adult*, Dr. Marc Angel[9] describes adults who have lost their parents as "adult orphans." This seemingly paradoxical label captures the ways in which adult status and stature can be dramatically informed by past connections to our most important early caregivers, our parents. Adults bring both reason and experience (as adults) and old anxieties and conflicts (as "orphans") in negotiating the complex adult world without the concrete anchor of living parents.

Employer-parents also straddle two worlds in the parent–caregiver relationship. As employers they must realistically focus on the concrete issues of schedule, pay, work responsibilities, autonomy, and control that are a necessary part of the parent–caregiver working arrangement. However, employer-parents, as parents, experience their relationship with the caregivers of their children in all of the drama, emotional binds, and ambivalent feelings that stem from their own childhood experiences with their own parents.

Likewise, employee-caregivers expect a professional approach to the arrangement and handling of all aspects of their work structure and environment. But employee-caregivers, as caregivers, feel all of the emotional tugs, past and present, that get stirred up when one is entrusted with the care and nurturing of children. In the corporate workplace, employees' struggles with their peers and supervisors often mirror their own personality struggles from their families of origin.[10]

ANNA, A PARENT, AND DEENA, A CAREGIVER: "YOU BE MY NETWORK, AND I'LL BE YOURS"

Anna noted that when she was looking for a caregiver for her daughter Ella, she wanted someone who was about her own age (late 30s) who had her own "good kids." It was also attractive to her when she first met Deena (who was ultimately to be Ella's caregiver) that she had a large, supportive, loving, and hard-working extended family—a network.

The interviewer listened for the less obvious (i.e., the more unconscious) pulls that might be involved in making these choices. Specifically, what were the qualities of the caregiver and her life that appeared to resonate with Anna's own needs and wishes for herself and her baby in forging and then maintaining this interrelationship with a caregiver?

Anna described her own mother as a teenage mother (like Deena), but with a dramatic history of stress and trauma from World War II. Her mother came to this country following the war and later married in an arranged but happy union. Anna remembered her mother's thirtieth birthday, celebrated without her father who had died four years earlier (when she was 8) from injuries sustained in a car accident. She noted that her connection with mother was particularly close. But there were aspects of her mother's history that loomed as a large, yet silent, presence in the story of Anna and Deena's relationship. Anna described her mother's escape from the Warsaw ghetto in 1938 with her family, thanks to her grandfather's vision, bravery, and stamina. Their journey took them through Russia in work camps, and included separations in orphanages. They also assisted numerous others in facing their fears by leaving their homes rather than waiting captive in Poland.

The First Crisis Point: Triumphs and Frustrations, Past and Present

Anna worked to duplicate this feeling of extended family with the caregiver (i.e., she wanted to be sure that she had a supportive, extended family). Consciously, she noted she was hoping that the caregiver's life included a support network in order to make her own life less complex. The strength and meaning of a complementary pull arose early on in a crisis in both their lives.

Two events ensued within a year after Deena began to work for Anna—Deena's pregnancy and birth of her own daughter, and only a few months later, Deena's illness requiring emergency surgery and a number of weeks off. Anna felt she could have let her go at that point but she "couldn't just leave her." This situation tapped into Anna's own unconscious needs to mother, and perhaps in connection with her past, to not leave Deena behind—to be her network, as her grandfather had been to so many. Anna noted that she made sure that Deena got the best care and kept the connection going by bringing Ella to see her, making do by using some of her own vacation time, coverage by her husband, and perhaps (unconsciously) and most importantly, through temporarily hiring Deena's sister who had come to the United States for an extended vacation (i.e., the network).

On a conscious level, it appealed to Anna that there was a warm, extended family available to Deena. On an unconscious level, Anna may have felt that aspects of Deena's life (i.e., being a single parent like Anna's mother was in her childhood) would affect Anna and Ella and her husband as well. Anna described an acute awareness that Deena allows her to do her professional work, assured that Ella's needs are met when she is away. At other moments, however, she was acutely aware of a reversal of those roles. She described a current situation that seemed to capture the conscious and unconscious dynamics and personal history being played out in the present.

The Second Crisis Point: Keeping It Working

Anna noted that Deena had asked for a personal day to attend her own daughter's high school graduation: "How could I deny such a request?" Anna added sadly that she had to miss Ella's preschool end of the year party due to her own work. She noted, "I don't have the kind of job where someone would be so understanding or take over for me so readily." Anna had mixed feelings of irritation, envy, as well as pride in being able to be Deena's network. She understood how important a high school graduation was, and she was pleased to give this moment to Deena.

This vignette captures the subtle interplay of consciously driven criteria for selection of a caregiver and equally compelling personal dynamics that spring from the unconscious (i.e., one's own emotional history). At one point in the interview, Anna noted that Deena had to leave her daughter when she was 8 in order to come to the United States for work, helping her daughter to immigrate several years ago when she was a teen. It was striking that Anna had lost her father at the same age that Deena's daughter had, in essence, "lost" Deena. Anna's need for a secure network, her sensitivity to issues of separation and loss, and her intuitive grasp of the importance of ongoing connections for young children all helped to forge an empathic connection (identification) with Deena's needs in this regard. This empathic connection allowed for a continuation in the good-enough relationship, which was in Ella's best interest at important points in her psychological and emotional development, such as late in her first year when initial exploration and tentative separations from one's first emotional connections occur, and later when she was making the transition to kindergarten. While another mother might have handled the initial crisis—Deena's surgery—in another way, this was the way that this pair had come together and worked through a crisis in their relationship.

A TIP FROM A PARENT AND A CAREGIVER: LIVE AND LET LIVE

Another working mother, Marcia, reflected on the reasons for the successful relationship she had had with her children's caregiver, Janice, for fourteen years: "We're good people to work for—money and things—and we're pleasant to be around." Marcia recognized that caregiving was not like being a secretary. Indeed, she appreciated that it was a much more demanding role: "She's on duty from 7 A.M. to 7 P.M." She described a give-and-take between them in terms of what Janice must do and what she could let go, depending on the children's needs and her own on a given day. Marcia knew that Janice was very dependable and responsible. She admired her common sense and her devotion to the two boys: "I can count on her to do the right thing." Even as she spoke of their having very little in common (education, economic status, cultural background, for example), Marcia added: "It's clear that she cares a great deal about the boys and their growth."

While these women came from very different worlds in almost every way, they shared two very important things. Both loved these children and both were working women who had to balance the responsibilities of home and work. They had had their share of ups and downs together, but they found it possible to make allowances for each other— one as an employer and the other as employee. There was an ongoing connection, like an extended family. These women needed each other and they knew it. Each sensed the limit and extent of the other's wish and need to be self-revealing. Boundaries were honored in the relationship.

7

Maintaining a Good-Enough Relationship

Once you've gotten through the hurdle of finding some-one you can trust, how do you deal with the inevitable struggles? Here are two crucial aspects of this ongoing job:

- Fostering communication: This requires a two-pronged approach. First, parents (and caregivers) must look internally, to themselves, their own emo-tional reactions, past history, and role in the day-to-day frustrations and triumphs of caring for the chil-dren. Second, each must look externally, to try to understand the position of the other.
- Developing the extended familial space: This involves a genuine stance of mutual concern for the caregiver by the parents, and for the parents by the caregiver. Ideally, the relationship should be a collaboration. This collaboration is a mutual agreement that the bottom line in all negotiations is what's best for the child. The space created for this mutuality is ulti-mately the parent's responsibility.

FOSTERING COMMUNICATION

To work successfully, both partners in this collaborative effort must recognize that open communication between them is essential. Parents and caregivers may vary greatly in their ability to examine their own issues and concerns, and to empathize with the issues and concerns of another. Two people can build considerable good will and increased openness when they simply acknowledge to one another that (1) each is trying to take responsibility for their own actions and their own role in the relationship, and (2) each is trying to consider the other person's side as well.

Stephen R. Covey, author of the international best-seller, *The Seven Habits of Highly Effective People*,[1] describes a simple yet powerful way to conceptualize the spirit of this approach to effective relationships with others. He notes, in keeping with our view here, that an inner awareness of our own needs, motivations, and perceptions is the essential first step in attempts to manage interpersonal struggles. Avoiding this crucial step only leaves the "underlying chronic problems untouched to fester and resurface time and again." Covey's paradigm for the seven habits rests upon a core fact of human relationships: While we are all, in reality, mutually interdependent, our personal levels of maturity may vary greatly. Because of our own internal struggles, we may still feel tied to others in a dependent interpersonal stance. We may have moved on to a more independent position, where at extremes we may seek to deny any need for others, always taking charge or pulling rank. In terms of real maturity, we may have arrived at the point that we have a true understanding of how we are mutually interdependent in our relationships.

We recognize that the parent–caregiver relationship, by the very nature of its functions, engenders feelings of dependency in parents and caregivers. Thus, in addition to a parent's or caregiver's individual level of maturity, there is this other hurdle—the real dependency that arises when lives are inextricably linked, as they are for parents and caregivers in the extended familial space. This is, again, the central paradox in understanding and managing the relationship between parents and caregivers. The fulcrum of this healthy, interdependent relationship consists of this active process of internal individual work along with the external empathic consideration of others.

Here's how two parents described how they managed their relationship with their au pair. The father was emphatic about his need for an independent stance when problems arise:

> The most important thing is not to be afraid to be direct and clear—laying out what you expect, what you want, what displeases you—as difficult as that might be. I wouldn't want a 40-year-old who is set in her own ways about taking care of the kids. Au pairs are more malleable. Maybe that isn't so diplomatic, but it works.

As the mother rolled her eyes, she added her more interdependent view:

> But relationships can be fragile, particularly at the beginning. You have to build trust. It's like any human relationship. Maybe it's especially true with live-ins. They are in your home. They can really feel like family. One au pair was taking the car out later than her curfew. When my husband confronted her, she started to cry and then avoided him for weeks. I said to her later, "You're part of the family. We have rules. There are good reasons for them. We're responsible for your well-being, and you are responsible for our children's well-being." It kind of felt like a role reversal—like we were caring for our child, even though she's 19. Sometimes it's like having your own teenager in the house.

This relationship worked, in part, because husband and wife complemented each other in their approach to their au pair.

Look to Yourself: The Internal Work

Many parents and caregivers described some awareness that things in the relationship were either working or stressful. Typically, most had only fragmented understanding as to why. Some had a pat explanation for every point of conflict. For example, some parents were described by caregivers as controllers, and some caregivers were described by parents as rigid or passive-aggressive, saying one thing and then doing another. Often, parents and caregivers tended to let things slide. All of these situations—from the vague sense of tension or stress to the more obvious crises and struggles that can arise—require an active process of internal and external exploration.

Frequently, parents and caregivers made use of informal, supportive networks in dealing with their problems. Caregivers tend to form groups of peers that parallel the social structures that one finds in corporate work settings. Parents talk with other parents in similar situations who know about issues that arise in negotiating these difficult relationships.

These informal groups provide both a useful outlet for frustrations as well as a place for trial thoughts and actions—"thinking out loud" with friends on a particularly stressful issue in the relationship. Yet we noted a tendency among caregivers and parents alike to externalize responsibility for all the difficulty to the other in the relationship: "It's her fault, not mine!" The need to seek out other people's opinions to confirm our own perceptions can be problematic.

Here are some of the signals that a crisis may be brewing:

- Repetitive patterns: It's the same old song with a familiar beat.
- Worrying: You find yourself retracing your thoughts and steps in an obsessive way.

- Confusion about what to think, do, or say.
- Struggling over your role in the relationship: You find yourself "drawing a line in the sand" or "showing who's the boss."

When struggling in an interpersonal situation, people protect themselves from anxiety over what might happen by using emotional shields or defenses. For example, we might:

- Put the blame on the other person.
- Become inflexible, failing to see the other person's side.
- On the surface, act as if nothing is wrong and shrug off any bad feelings.
- Bend over backward in accepting the other's position.
- "Make nice" or let things slide.

Whenever we note something brewing, our first step should be to look to ourselves:

- Stop, step back, and reflect: Stop and take a break from the struggle. Take a step back to observe and reflect on the situation. If this type of struggle feels familiar, when have you been in this situation before? Look for similar threads.
- What is the emotional struggle for you in this surface issue? Keep an eye on the typical human reactions—especially for mothers and caregivers, such as the often overlooked connections of jealousy, competition, and control over the special care that the child is getting from two mothering figures.
- Think through your role in the parent–caregiver relationship: Where do you and the caregiver stand on the continuum of employer–employee and "family" member? Is there a good flexible balance between these positions, or does the tension seem to be com-

ing from some struggle around extremes on this continuum?

- Where do you stand in terms of feeling dependent or independent? Do you feel at the mercy of one another, or do you find yourself operating without a collaborative stance?
- What steps can you take to develop or restore a feeling of mutual interdependence with the caregiver (or the caregiver with the parent)?
- How can you use trusted others who know you to help identify your patterns when you feel stuck?

Here is an example of how one mother addressed an ongoing struggle with her daughter's caregiver. It reveals the internal work she did as well as the use to which she put her husband's feedback.

Monica, a mother, seemed to know important aspects of her dynamics but was stuck in terms of her ability to make the leap to using this insight. Describing repeated struggles over how Celeste, her daughter's caregiver, structured her day, she finally noted, "I'm a control freak." Monica complained of failed attempts to get Celeste to follow her busy daily schedule of suggested outings, such as museum trips, library visits, and play dates, as well as craft activities at home. Celeste always fell short of Monica's expectations for the stimulation she felt her daughter needed in her absence. Monica noted, "I just don't want her to be bored, sitting around without an interested adult nearby." In recounting Celeste's stony silences following Monica's "reasonable attempts" to talk about what she expected Celeste to do with the schedule, Monica remembered something her husband had said: "Monica, no one can be you, and no one can be perfect." At this point in the interview, one of the authors recalled that Monica had described, in idealized terms, a housekeeper named Vera who had worked for her family and spent many hours playing games and talking with her in her childhood. We asked if anyone could ever be as good as Vera. Monica fell silent for a moment. Then, with a bittersweet smile, she responded, "No. No one can be Vera." It seems so simple for a third party to see from the outside, yet it is another matter to look for these patterns for oneself.

Once Monica was aware that she had been expecting Celeste to be Vera, she was able to let go of her insistence on controlling the caregiver's schedule exactly. When she thought about firing Celeste, she realized her disappointment was due in part to her mental image of Vera not dovetailing with the reality of Celeste. Without the shadow of this ideal image, Monica was able to appreciate important aspects of her relationship with Celeste and the way she was taking care of her daughter. "When I leave in the morning, I never worry for a moment that she isn't in safe and competent hands." She was also able to recall less than ideal aspects of Vera's work in her childhood home. "My parents were always talking about firing her, and we would protest. They said she was there to help as a housekeeper, but spent most of her time hanging out with us. I remember saying to my mother, "Why does the house have to be so clean, anyway?" At this point, Monica's own struggles with her need for the house to be kept fanatically clean by Celeste was too far removed from her awareness to temper those expectations.

It would have been helpful for Monica if she were able to connect her disappointment with Celeste's performance and her thoughts of firing her to her childhood experience with Vera and her own mother as data in assessing the realistic need (if any) to fire this caregiver. In a sense, that was then; this is now. Vera was Vera.

This is Celeste. She will never be Vera. The question for Monica to ask herself is, Can I accept Celeste as she is and live with her? Without realizing it, Monica had been comparing Celeste to Vera, always finding her coming up short. This can wreak havoc on any relationship. The important question should be, Is she doing a good enough job as a caregiver in her own right based on the criteria important to the mother?

Empathize: The External Work

Putting ourselves in someone else's shoes can be a difficult task, especially when we are in conflict with her. We have a major stake in *our* view, *our* thoughts, and *our* feelings. This was the case with Monica, the mother embroiled in a struggle for control of the schedule with Celeste, her daughter's caregiver. Monica viewed Celeste's stony silences as an example of her rigidity, nothing more. It was difficult for Monica to see her own role (the internal work) and to consider Celeste's perspective (the external work). Trying to see things from Celeste's vantage point felt like a threat to Monica's position.

Here are some ways in which the necessary shift to view an interpersonal situation from the vantage point of another person can feel problematic:

- We may feel that we've lost the battle.
- We can feel that we've surrendered part of ourselves if we let go of our convictions, even for a moment.
- We can feel that we may become a patsy and leave ourselves open to manipulation.
- We may feel that taking a closer look at someone else's thoughts and feelings is threatening to how we view our own.

Colloquial phrases speak of empathy: "Walk a mile in her shoes," or "Try to understand where she is coming from." We note that we may have similar struggles or foibles when we say, "People who live in glass houses shouldn't throw stones."

Considering the position of the caregiver (for parents) or the parents (for caregivers) may put each in a vulnerable spot. Parents can feel that their wishes as employer-parents must be acknowledged, accepted, and followed. They may feel that their view is nonnegotiable. Employee-caregivers, from their perspective, can feel a personal stake in the care of the children and management of the household, so they take a stand. Often, just when parents and caregivers are locked in conflict, there is a marked tendency to lose any empathic connection to one another. We suggest the following ways for parents to enter into the world of the caregiver (and caregivers to consider the parent's position). These active attempts to foster communication for collaborative problem solving are at the core of this empathic external work:

- *Imagine yourself in the shoes of the other person.* Visualize their daily routine.[2] For parents, this means imagining your caregiver leaving her home and responsibilities to come to yours. In your mind, run through what that day might be like. Remind yourself of how you can feel after a day of juggling child care responsibilities. Recall how often your personal needs are not met. Consider how necessary it is for you to have a break from child care responsibilities.

- *Draw on your reservoir of good feeling in the relationship.* Take time to consider your feelings toward this person at other moments. Is there more good feeling than bad feeling in the relationship reservoir?[3] This is not to say that you should overlook the issue at hand or your feelings about it. Rather, it is an attempt to put things in proper perspective.

- *Put the other at ease.* The focus should be on keeping the positive aspects of the relationship in the forefront. We can then ease into the criticism or concern. We might say, "I can understand why you felt that taking Sally with you to run your errand during her nap time was your only option. I feel strongly that she needs her nap in her crib, not in the stroller. Was there another time you could have run that errand?"

- *Enlist the assistance of the other in a collaborative spirit.* The focus should be on addressing a problem to find a mutual solution. It is important to let go of the notion that the solution has to come via some directive from the parent. Ideally, it should be arrived at together, or at least with the input of both parties in the relationship. Asking someone what she thinks is a powerful collaborative tool.[4] But there is an important caveat here: you can't feign interest in someone else's perspective. It has to be genuine.

One mother described the way she empathized with her daughter's caregiver around a painful reality of their working relationship. Each of them was faced with the fact that they had to work during their child's first week of kindergarten.

I felt guilty that I was taking the caregiver from her own child due to her work schedule. Her work involved taking my daughter to that first week of school because I had to work. I also felt envious that she is able to spend this special time with my daughter. It all felt so crazy-making. So I just told her that directly. I looked at her that first morning and said, "This is the plight of the working parent. It stinks sometimes." She smiled, then we both laughed and hugged and started to cry. I felt so close to her. But somehow that week, I had some breathing space in my schedule. I would be able to bring my daughter to

school one of the mornings. As soon as I found out, I called
the caregiver. I told her that we could both do what we
really wanted and needed to do for ourselves that next
morning.

How to Talk So People Can Hear

In our interviews we heard how parents and caregivers
alike felt a compelling need to make the other "listen,"
rather than hear the other person's perspective. Each felt it
imperative that the other see things her way. We suggest
that a slight shift in emphasis—talking so people can hear—
is crucial in negotiating the parent–caregiver relationship.[5]

In matters where there is objectively a potential for
harm or great risk, parents must clearly state what they
want. For example, if a caregiver fails to use a safety belt
for the children when riding in a cab, or frequently arrives
late to pick up a child from school, or fails to provide any
stimulation other than television, or uses too many time-
outs unnecessarily, these failures must be dealt with directly. When caregivers' job responsibilities become
conflictual, or too burdensome, or their salary is not paid
on time, lines must be drawn. For example, parents may
demand to see proof that their toddler is doing arts and
crafts during the day and also expect housekeeping, cooking, and shopping to be done. Addressing situations like
these, however stressful, need not be problematic.

Rather, it is within the day-to-day details of caring for
children that communication often breaks down. Even
parents and caregivers who see themselves as easygoing
and diplomatic in their dealings with others can find themselves pulling rank or, at the other extreme, letting things
slide. Here we present some useful tools for (1) heading off
the extreme struggles before they fester, and (2) communicating in the most effective manner for the sake of the relationship.

- *Keep an active dialogue going.* Ideally, each day should include at least a 10-minute discussion of the day's events and any concerns, and a review of the schedule. Most importantly, these exchanges allow for a transition for the child, the caregiver, and the parent in their interrelationship. This "changing of the guard" signals to all parties that something is different, and acknowledges the presence and importance of both caregiver and the parent. Early in the relationship, and when dealing with infants and young children, more time may be needed to make these transitions.

  In addition, status meetings of at least twenty minutes should be scheduled into the caregiver's workday on a regular (typically weekly) basis. This helps to reinforce and reward current efforts, and assists in dealing with any ongoing problems and in discussing any developmental changes that may be occurring with the children. Making this meeting a priority communicates the value that parents place on a collaborative relationship. In this way, both parents and caregivers will feel listened to, respected, and considered.

- *Intervene effectively.* At times we may get so irritated or angry that we can't help attacking. At these moments it may be best to take a "time out" to consider what is involved for each person. However, waiting too long after an event can make it hard to recall accurately. It may also allow for protective "forgetting" to set in. Ideally, somewhere between the heat of the moment and the cold of forgetting is a good time to intervene effectively.

- *Say something positive.* A general rule for addressing problems and giving constructive feedback: first say something positive that someone has been doing, and then mention the concern that you would like to address.[6] The more flexible you are with what you want to see improved or changed, and the more you can enlist the other person on ideas to make this change, the better the collaboration.

- *Presume innocence.* Try to address the other person with an open mind. You will accomplish much more with a genuine interest in and request for information than by becoming a grand inquisitor with your first question.

- *Do the hard part first.* Address the topic of concern first in the conversation. We tend to leave the hard stuff for the end of conversations, when it may get treated with less concern and attention than we had intended. We may also inadvertently give the message that the concern is an afterthought.

- *Focus on the "I," not the "you."* Whenever describing a difficult situation, if we describe the effect someone else's behavior has on us (or in this case on our children or in the household space), it is typically easier to hear.[7]

- *Provide support for areas of concern.* Look for opportunities to exhibit or model preferred ways to handle various problem areas.

- *Catch someone doing good and let them know about it.* Letting someone know that you notice and appreciate her work, particularly something that has been discussed where you see a change has been made, is invaluable. Do more than simply saying thanks; make a specific reference to what she has been doing.

- *Pick your battles.* We all do this in our intimate relationships. But this must be an active decision-making process and ideally should reflect a shift, however subtle, from our expectations. This shift in expecta-

tions must come from our internal acknowledgment
of our own unrealistic needs from our past, or from
an acceptance that the caregiver may not be able to
provide something we now deem unessential. This is
different from letting things slide.

• *Avoid situations of total dependence.* Address early on
the reality that there will be times when parents and
caregivers need backup due to the complexities in
their lives. Doing this early on and collaborating on
this effort will reduce the panic that can ensue.

• *Turn turf wars into collaborative efforts.* This is perhaps the most difficult perspective to shift. Turf wars
are struggles played out in the arena of the day-to-
day care of the children where control gets exerted.
Parents and caregivers can often feel, in their own
ways, either dependent on each other, or totally independent and inconsiderate of the other (often to
counter feelings of dependency). Fostering a sense of
interdependence in the relationship—a mutual responsibility and balance of each other's needs—helps
things work better for all concerned.

DEVELOPING THE EXTENDED
FAMILIAL SPACE

"Somehow, everybody ends up helping out everybody else
with everything," said a parent, reflecting on the nature
of the collaboration between parents and caregivers in creating the extended familial space.

Throughout this book we have described ways in which
the extension of the familial space to include the caregiver
creates a crisis—a potential for conflict as well as an opportunity for adaptation and growth. Parents who acknowledge the importance of the caregiver's role in the growth
and development of their children as well as in their day-

to-day family life take a crucial first step in forging a working relationship. This crucial first step sets the tone and
allows for the development of the extended familial space
both literally (in the household) and figuratively (as an
emotional connection). When parents make this step, they
provide for the possibility of creative collaboration. Viewing
the relationship through this prism is a difficult but worth-
while exercise. It is also an ideal—something to strive for.

In our culture, we are accustomed to express appreciation in concrete ways, with gifts, courtesies, thank yous,
and so on. Too often we give such appreciation in perfunctory ways. But you can't fake concern for others. There is
no formula for showing sincere interest or consideration.
A collaborative spirit isn't something we can perform using a checklist or a bag of tricks. We know intuitively when
people treat us with respect and when people are sincere.
When we approach others with the intention to ingratiate
ourselves, or to get something back in return, we keep a
silent scorecard that, over time, can become a deafening
clamor of expectations.

The Buck Stops Here: Ultimate Responsibility

Parents understandably feel that since they are contract-
ing for child care and/or household assistance, everything
should be provided for as explicitly agreed to in the employer–employee contract. But it is in the day-to-day application of this contract, the collaborative spirit, that the
relationship can either flourish or fester. It is here where
the paradoxical relationship lives. It is the place where
parents are also employers and caregivers are also like
members of the family.

But there are two realities of the parent–caregiver relationship that are undeniable. First, parents, by their status as employers and socioeconomic level, are holding the
upper hand in terms of the interpersonal power in the re-

lationship. Second, by virtue of their parental bond and responsibility, parents have the greatest investment in providing an optimal developmental experience for their children. It is for these reasons that the ultimate responsibility for fostering and safeguarding this collaborative spirit rests with the parents. For their part, caregivers, as professionals, must strive to behave in a way that befits their role and fosters self-esteem in their job.

The Collaborative Spirit

Many parents and caregivers described the ways in which a spirit of collaboration was begun and maintained in their working relationship. Most agreed that regular transitional and ongoing contact was very important. Others underscored (from both sides) the importance of the parents always paying the caregiver on time. Some parents spoke of trying to be sensitive to their caregiver's work load and monitoring her need for understandable work breaks. Some caregivers spoke of their awareness of the pulse of the family life. They also were aware that their presence was paradoxically an asset and a potential interference in the core family life. Parents and caregivers, in the best of these relationships, described a "live and let live" attitude. They seemed committed to help each other's lives work.

Cynthia, a single mother, described the many ways in which she worked to create an extended familial space with her daughter's caregivers, YueHua and her husband DeGui:

> A friend of mine had come to visit for the weekend. YueHua and DeGui had some company that afternoon, visiting for tea in the living room. So my daughter Sara, my friend, and I went up to my master bedroom and watched television. She said, "I don't get this . . . this is your house, why aren't we in the living room?" Well, I just explained that we were three people and they were six people. This isn't a master–servant relationship. They had the critical mass

so they got the larger space that afternoon. Most people don't think that way. But if you do think that way, the people who work for you like you. That's how you get through the difficult discussions about differences in child rearing and you can still deal with each other.

YueHua and DeGui also described their sense of why things worked for them. They noted how they were able to live together and juggle their employment and personal relationship as "family" to one another:

> In China there is an expression, "Two separate sides are very good, but put together, things are much better!" First of all, Cynthia is a nice lady. She is outspoken and we are comfortable with that and her personality. She helps us a lot. Not just that we take care of Sara. She wants to help. She helps us with writing our English. She is not like a boss. It is very equal. She is a good friend. If we think about the relationship as just employer–employee, work, pay— the relationship cannot last so long. Many families have child care only months or maybe a year or two.
>
> When we think like a family, we treat each other with respect, not like an employer–employee. Like a family, you will take care of each other. It is both sides.

There was also a healthy, good-natured sense of interplay at moments when things weren't so ideal. DeGui said,

> Sometimes, I admit, I am lazy around the house. I don't get to my fixing projects. YueHua, my wife, complains. Sometimes Cynthia complains, too: "DeGui, you are so lazy sometimes!" I don't mind, she's right. You never mind when you feel like family. So she reminds me of something I am getting behind in and I get to it. Cynthia is very busy and she always is doing her part in the household. So I have to do my part, too. This is only fair.

Another mother described the delicate and subtle way in which her 3-year-old daughter made the transition from her day with her nanny to her reunion in the early evening with mother. Both mother and caregiver, through a mutual understanding in their relationship, had come to negotiate these moments in a way that allowed for this adaptive and crucial transition:

> One evening recently I came in and found Lana on Marta's lap. Lana looked up and gave me a smile and Marta continued to read the book they were in the middle of at the moment. She said, "You sit, Mamma, you listen, Mamma." So I sat nearby and listened. Lana motioned for me to come closer after a few minutes, so I did. Then she slowly stretched out her leg and rested her foot on my leg. After they finished the book, she just sort of slid over onto my lap.

This child is lucky. She has a mother and caregiver who let her make the switch in her own way and at her own pace.

TRUST

"It's like starting to date a divorced man. You always find yourself wondering where have they been, what were they really up to before?" This is how one mother succinctly described her anxieties about having a new caregiver, a stranger in her home.

Electronic devices that monitor caregivers serve an important function when parents suspect neglect and are unable to check their caregiver's child care through unscheduled drop-ins, especially early in the relationship. But measuring the quality of attachment and care, whether a caregiver is good enough, is, unfortunately, a much more complicated task than electronic devices can address. As one parent noted, "I'd hate to have someone record me when I'm having a bad parenting moment." Choosing a trustworthy caregiver for their child is one of the most important decisions parents have to make. The correctness of their decision affects their working relationship. Trust develops over time.

Lillian, a Mother, and Maura, a Caregiver: "Where Are You When I Need You?"

Maura had been out of work for several weeks due to the severe illness of her own son, and Lillian, her employer, had been very sympathetic and accommodating. Maura could not return full time at first, so Lillian had hired Kathleen, a part-time caregiver that she knew to be trustworthy, for her 6-year-old son, Michael, who had been cared for by Maura since birth. A crisis arose between Lillian and Maura when she first made a tentative return, which seemed to capture an ongoing dynamic noted silently but never directly addressed by Lillian.

The Third Crisis Point: Half Truths or Total Deceptions?

Maura seemed happy to be back at work. But she was tense and irritated as she approached Lillian with some upsetting news. Maura said, "I went into my closet in the study where I keep some of my personal things. I know I left fifty dollars in my jar in there three weeks ago. It's gone. Did Kathleen use that space for her things last week?" Knowing Kathleen as she did, Lillian did not believe that she would have stolen anyone's money. Lillian simply could not believe Maura.

Lillian noted, "I remembered how many times Maura had a good-natured yet possessive air in the house when a delivery would come or a workman would be there. It actually left me with a sense of security that she felt attached and in charge as if treating this space and our home as she would her own. But this felt strange and out of bounds." Lillian recalled that she had quickly said that she couldn't imagine that Kathleen would have taken the money. Maura simply denied that she had accused Kathleen. "I knew she had accused Kathleen, but I could sense that something very distressing was happening for Maura at the moment and she couldn't comprehend it. I just kept it to myself for the moment."

Maura had felt vulnerable in her own unavailability to the family and had momentarily forgotten the strength of the family's attachment to her (i.e., the six years) despite the recent acknowledgment of her genuine importance to the family that was shown through the flexibility and care extended to her own ill child. Lillian not only had given her time off, but had helped her find the best possible medical care for her child. There was no question in Lillian's mind about doing these things. Lillian noted matter of factly, "It felt reflexive. She is family." This feeling of attachment and care on Lillian's part, which was at odds with Maura's internal struggle, ended when Maura's "lie" about Kathleen had fueled Lillian's anger. "I hated how controlling and mean-spirited Maura was in her accusation of Kathleen. When I caught her in the lie about Kathleen and then she even denied the accusation, I thought does she take me for an idiot or a patsy?" Lillian noted, "I felt like I had bent over backward for her and now she was undermining my attempt to get some temporary assistance for myself with Michael at a very busy time in my work life and at home."

The dynamic was a deep and enduring one for Maura, who was a good caregiver and employee and had reacted to a particular stressor with a characteristic response. She felt fearful of her own dependency on this family and needed to reassert what she felt was her tenuous position in the only way that dynamically fit the moment for her. Kathleen was available right now and Maura had proven herself less so and therefore less than ideal. Lillian speculated about Maura's fierce loyalty yet sense of insecurity at times in the household: "I remembered that she was the middle child of a big Irish family and her value I think must have rested, in her mind, on how consistent and hard working she could be. I don't think it's easy for her to take what she needs, but she clearly feels threatened when she allows herself some flexibility." This case is a wonderful example of how a good-enough relationship between parent and caregiver is contingent on both parties having the capacity for "object constancy"—the positive stable conceptualization of, and attachment to, another person and all of his or her characteristic ways of thinking, feeling, and being despite an inability to provide for our every need at a given moment.[8]

If the parties involved can work out their issues, this bodes well for the future for the child who needs to learn, by example, to integrate both positive and negative, loving and hating feelings about important persons in one's world. Only then can the child experience these important others as consistently available, and in turn develop a solid sense of oneself as capable in facing life's inevitable frustrations.

When Lillian felt overwhelmed, she became aware of the need to talk this out. This was a crucial part of why the intervention succeeded. Lillian's capacity to talk about her feelings with a trusted friend helped her to gain the perspective to deal with the situation clearly. This included her ability to identify some of what might be going on for Maura. Lillian noted, "Nine out of ten people might have fired her right on the spot if they just looked at this as lying or stealing by an employee."

Carla, a Mother: Taking a Leap of Faith

Carla described an essentially good-enough relationship with her 3-year-old son's caregiver, Nellie. Carla acknowledged a range of positive and negative feelings about Nellie, including a keen sense of her own ambivalent feelings about relinquishing control of her son's care during the day and entrusting Nellie with the run of the household. Carla was thoughtful and insightful. She noted with pride her methods of dealing with her feelings and in managing Nellie effectively. "I know her pretty well—how proper and private she is and how she can become sullen and sensitive if she feels criticized."

Shortly after the initial interview, one of the interviewers received a call from Carla. "I'm so furious. I just picked up my monthly tab from the pharmacy and found some nail polish had been charged. I don't even use the stuff." As we began to talk about the feeling of betrayal that seemed to fuel this anger, it became clear that an idealized (and unspoken) image of Nellie had come in conflict with reality in the form of this betrayal. As Carla became more aware of her loss of this ideal, she began to talk of her anger and her underlying concerns: "I had a moment where I thought—that's it, she can't be trusted with my child, either."

She began to think about her work and how soothing the thought of Nellie's trustworthness had been to her. After allowing these feelings to settle into the greater perspective of the good-enough relationship with her son's caregiver, she chuckled and noted, "If I had a dime for every time I took a jar of whiteout home, I'd be a rich woman." Her ability to make the connection to her loss of this ideal image and to feel her anger helped her to connect empathically to what it means at certain moments to be an employee (i.e., to make the connection of nail polish and whiteout) and to reestablish her perspective and ongoing attachment to Nellie as the essentially good-enough caregiver that she knew her to be.

8
Calling It Quits

Relationships end. The emotional connection between "endings" and "death" conjures up anxiety for people, perhaps intense anxiety, depending on one's personal history of separation and loss and how these endings were acknowledged and negotiated.

When an important relationship ends, our world can feel strange and empty. The physical absence of a central person may alter our day-to-day existence dramatically. We may be left without needed supports, making our lives more stressful. We may feel empty ourselves, as if we've lost a part of ourselves. We may numb ourselves to the loss, acting at times as if nothing had changed, moving ahead seemingly without feelings. In more extreme cases, loss of an important relationship may feel like a death. On the other end of the spectrum, endings to relationships can feel like a welcomed relief, as when a relationship has felt burdensome, or worse, abusive.

When parents and caregivers end their formal relationship, there is a complex mix of such feelings. In many cases, the loss of someone who has been a support to the entire family may leave parents and children in a state of confusion or mourning. In other cases, where there has been more tension and misalignment between the parents and caregivers, ending the relationship may be a relief. Parents can feel guilty terminating the working arrangements with their caregiver, especially if she does not yet have another job. Here, as in every aspect of the caregiver–parent relationship, we found individual styles of recognizing, addressing, and coping with these feelings of loss, anger, and guilt that inevitably come when the relationship ends.

In the best-case scenario, for both parents and caregivers, endings are planned—either programmed from the start or addressed directly when they are imminent. This is most obvious in the case of au pairs, who contract for a year of work. The clear-cut, programmed ending to the au pair contract may be part of the appeal of the arrangement for many parents. While parents and au pairs have described a conscious sense of relief about this inherent time boundary, we noted signs of emotional struggles and continued ties in many of these time-bound relationships. With other in-home caregivers, the relationship may end when families or caregivers move or change jobs. Long-standing relationships often end gradually when the inevitable happens—the children enter school and move toward greater independence outside the family unit.

In the typical-case scenario, endings are seemingly unplanned and happen abruptly. These unplanned endings are sometimes triggered by unavoidable circumstances in a person's life. More commonly, they are precipitated by troubles that have been brewing but have gone unaddressed. Often, even endings that can be anticipated and planned come as emotional upheavals in the guise of struggles around surface issues such as changes in pay, schedule, or job responsibilities.

In the worst-case scenario, the need for an emergency ending to the child care arrangement must be identified, evaluated, and dealt with directly, as when there is neglect or abuse. Although relatively rare, such situations are every parent's worst fear. There are also situations in which seemingly intractable struggles evolve between parents and caregivers. These are chronic points of irritation or mis-alignment in the relationship due to a bad match or some underlying personality issues for both parties. When such struggles in the relationship continue even after parents and caregivers have tried everything they can to make things better, ending the relationship is the only option that is in the best interests of the child.

We will deal first with the relatively rare worst-case scenario; these are situations in which a bad child care arrangement must end. Then we address the typical-case scenario; these endings are abrupt and unplanned. Finally, we describe the best-case scenario; these are endings that are planned, and allow for a process of separation and mourning that is necessary emotional work for children to learn, by example, from the adults who care for them.

THE EMERGENCY TERMINATION

One father struggled to sort out the difference between a problem caregiver and a parent's own conflicts:

> If a caregiver is screwed up, if she is not taking proper care, you're going to learn that sooner or later. Then you have to have the maturity and decisiveness to get that person out of your (and your child's) life. It's the other side, when the person is actually fine, objectively, and you're acting out your own concerns, your stuff—like conflicted feelings about having the caregiver in your child's life, or your own personality problems. Then you can end up taking it out on the caregiver.

How can you tell the difference between a problem caregiver and a parent's own personality conflicts that have made for intractable struggles in the relationship? How does one really know, in a given situation, that a caregiver arrangement must end? In Chapter 5 we outlined some of the ways in which old personality struggles can become stirred up in the parent–caregiver relationship. In Chapter 6 we described ways to optimize the chances that these old and problematic patterns don't determine (completely) the selection of a caregiver. In Chapter 7 we addressed typical struggles in the parent–caregiver relationship. We described ways to tell the difference between these old struggles and real issues that must be attended to (the internal work). We also described ways to optimize the relationship to maintain good lines of communication that allow for a healthy dialogue when the inevitable struggles arise (the external work).

There are times when an immediate break in the relationship is necessary or inevitable. While child abuse in child care settings is generally rare, and most abuse occurs within the family,[1] from and by family members or stepparents, parents using any child care arrangement must be aware of the signs and symptoms of neglect or abuse. Most often, parents find that when they acknowledge such fears and investigate their concerns more directly, they are enormously relieved and enlightened. The process of addressing these concerns forces parents to examine their children's child care needs more directly. It can also help them to empathize with the rigors of daily child responsibilities of caregivers. The key to preventing neglect and abuse by a caregiver lies in the parent's vigilance and involvement. It is also essential to forming a good-enough relationship with the caregiver.

When the Relationship is Less Than Good-Enough: How to Spot a Bad Child Care Arrangement

Bad child care arrangements fall generally within four categories that may overlap:

1. A caregiver (or parent) is *abusive:* By abuse, we mean, broadly, any act (typically resulting in injury) that adversely affects the development of the child. These ac-

tions may be physical abuse (resulting in bruises, fractures, or more severe injury), sexual abuse (from subtle inappropriate behavior to outright sexual contact), or psychological-emotional abuse (such as screaming rages, vicious belittling).

2. A caregiver (or parent) is *neglectful:* By neglect, we mean failure to perform basic, developmentally necessary caregiving functions. These are acts of omission that include, broadly, physical neglect (such as failure to provide for proper medical care, feeding, shelter/clothing/cleansing, and safety needs), and psychological-emotional neglect (such as failure to provide age-appropriate attention, stimulation, affection, comfort, and support). In most cases, true neglect is chronic, not an isolated event or momentary lapse in caregiving. As one example of neglect, a mother returned home unexpectedly during the day to find her child in the playpen, in a soaking-wet diaper, while the caregiver slept on the couch. As another example, a parent got a call from a neighbor who saw the au pair drinking a beer in the park at lunchtime while her toddler was too far away from her supervision.

3. A caregiver (or parent) is *very troubled:* For example, one mother described coming home to find her child's caregiver sitting in her underwear, acting as if nothing was inappropriate about it. Another mother told of a caregiver who had prevented her 6-year-old from using the computer; with further exploration, she discovered that the caregiver had a complex belief, outside of mainstream ideas, that children were being "controlled" by modern technology.

A more complicated picture arises when a caregiver (or parent) is unable to maintain the employer/employee–"family" balance that is necessary in the relationship. For example, one caregiver constantly and defiantly disregarded a parent's reasonable request that she first discuss any plans to take the child to places outside of the usual routine. Another caregiver was terminated after she became verbally abusive to the children's grandparents who arrived at the door unexpectedly to visit; this caregiver had lost perspective regarding her place in the child's life, since she felt the grandparents were not being respectful of her "special time" with the children.

4. There is an irreconcilable personality difference or *bad match* between the parent and the caregiver: For example, one parent, relieved at first by her caregiver's take charge style, found herself fearful of the caregiver's angry tirades whenever she made attempts to negotiate changing details of the child care arrangement. This mother felt she was always "walking on eggshells."

Signs from the Child–Caregiver Relationship

Parents (and caregivers as well) are often reluctant to acknowledge that a child is being neglected or abused in a child care arrangement. It is hard to believe that anyone would overlook these signs. But this knowledge may be too frightening to become fully aware of, too painful to admit. It may represent a worse fear that has been repressed. It may stir up intense feelings of rage, guilt, or remorse. Some parents may simply be unable to admit that someone they were so sure had provided good care might be guilty of neglect or responsible for some abuse. Such a mistake may feel like a blow to a parent's sense of control and personal efficacy.

The signs of neglect or abuse in child care arrangements may emerge from the child–caregiver relationship or from the parents' relationship with the caregiver. These signs are potential indicators, not foolproof evidence. There are a number of excellent references and resources available on this subject through federal agencies such as the National Clearinghouse on Child Abuse and Neglect Information.[2] Our main sources of information for this general overview of signs of neglect or abuse are the American Academy of Pediatrics guide, *Caring for Your Baby and Young Child*,[3] and James A. Monteleone's comprehensive text, *Recognition of Child Abuse for the Mandated Reporter*.[4]

Signs from the Children

Children communicate their distress in their relationship with their caregiver in ways that adults may not expect. How they communicate is very much a function of their age, their immediate life circumstances, and their individual personality style or temperament. Children can respond to a wide variety of stressors or traumas in typical ways. Preschoolers tend to show general stress reactions such as changes in basic and newly learned behavioral patterns such as eating and sleeping habits. They may lose control of learned bladder and bowel functions. They may also become more aggressive in their play, moody and withdrawn, or they may suffer from nightmares or terrors. Older children (of school age) may show difficulties with learning, attention, poor peer relations, moodiness, depression and anxiety, and a variety of vague somatic complaints. Here are some of the more specific indicators that may warrant immediate action and/or further investigation:

The Hard Signs—Abuse

These signs are always cause for concern. They necessitate immediate investigation and action.

Signs of physical abuse include repeated bumps and bruises that are unexplained, do not make logical sense, or are without signs of concern by the caregiver; older children who are frightened by being left with the caregiver; and reliable reports by trustworthy neighbors, friends, or professionals that an infant or child has been hit, verbally abused, or grossly neglected by the caregiver.

Signs of sexual abuse include unexplained urinary tract infections; sexually transmitted disease; unexplained genital or anal pains accompanied by irritation or bleeding; sexually provocative behavior, excessive masturbation, or exposing genitals, outside of what would be typically expected for that age; and extreme fear reactions to toileting, bathing, or changing clothes.

Signs of psychological-emotional abuse include extreme self-deprecating comments, actions, or self-harm; overly aggressive play; depression, loss of appetite, sleep disturbance, and night terrors that may include reference to the caregiver; extreme anxiety, fears outside of the typical developmental expectations; a beaten down, skittish, or agitated quality to interactions with others.

The Soft Signs—Neglect

These signs can often accompany physical abuse but may be the focus in cases of maltreatment or neglect.

Signs of physical neglect include in infants, a chronic, severe diaper rash without other explanations (such as diarrhea, flu); and in children, dirty clothes, or dirt on the body that does not come off in the bath.

Signs of psychological-emotional neglect include fussy, clingy, and cranky behavior; eating too much or too little; sleep disturbance, nightmares; strong emotional outbursts and tantrums; and loss of basic functions such as toileting.

Signs from the Caregiver

When you attempt to discuss these situations with the caregiver, particularly some of the soft signs, how does she respond? Does she notice these things, too? Does she have any ideas about what may be involved, or does she immediately (and relentlessly) become defensive, hostile, or aggressive? Do her explanations of what occurred make sense?

Is the caregiver unstable emotionally? Have you noticed a pattern of unrealistic expectations of the child's developmental level? Does the caregiver seem too distant, too possessive of the child, or too private in their relationship? Does she seem lethargic, moody, or preoccupied? Do you suspect that drugs may be involved? How does she refer to the child—by name or nickname, or impersonally?

Does the caregiver seem overly secretive (i.e., not simply private about personal details)? Does the caregiver exhibit sociopathic tendencies? For example, one parent described a caregiver who consistently wore new clothing, the latest fashion, that she would return after one wearing, apparently intimidating the salespeople into giving her a full refund. Another mother described a caregiver who had been responsible for stealing checks and a credit card, then forging the parent's signature. Still another reported that the level in the vodka bottle dropped over a period of weeks when neither parent had touched it.

Caveats

In cases of suspected psychological-emotional abuse or soft signs of neglect or maltreatment, the following extenuating circumstances are always important to consider:

- Can the current observations be explained any other way? For example, is the child experiencing a major life adjustment such as a divorce, loss of an important person or pet, a trauma, birth of a sibling, or adjustment to the start of a preschool program?
- Is the child, by nature and temperament, somewhat fussy (i.e., not an abrupt change from an ongoing state)?
- What developmental step is currently under way? For example, if a young toddler has a bump on his head reportedly from a fall when climbing, is this activity commensurate with his current skills? For some chil-

dren the "terrible twos" and the struggles around toilet training may be more accentuated. These struggles
are also dependent on their temperament, since some
children are more anxious by nature. Boys, in particular, may have more difficulty with bowel training. But
this should not be an excuse for a caregiver who cannot negotiate this difficult period without resorting to
maladaptive approaches, like verbal abuse, emotional
neglect, or, in the worst case, physical abuse. Regardless of a child's difficult temperament, it is the
caregiver's, and ultimately the parent's, job to adapt
her caregiving to the needs of the child.
- There is some indication that children who have
caregivers may have a more protracted stormy period
in terms of the typically expected emotional struggles
with control and autonomous behavior.[5] These "terrible twos" may well stretch into the threes and fours.
Likewise parents report that children seem to save
up their emotional struggles for the time they are with
their parents.

When there is a high index of suspicion, it is important
for parents to calmly increase their surveillance and investigation. Depending on the urgency of the situation, this
may involve simply dropping in unexpectedly, or asking
neighbors to do so. This should not become a witch hunt.
As more than one parent told us, caregivers can sometimes
become the scapegoat for things that parents cannot bear
to note in themselves. The main issue is to protect the child
first, while also assuring and safeguarding that the
caregiver is not unjustly accused.

Parents may opt for electronic surveillance to investigate
their gut-level concerns. One expert, Craig Erkus,[6] of Nanny
Check, Inc., a Long Island City (New York) agency special-
izing in undetectable electronic home surveillance, notes
that in typically 80 to 90 percent of cases, neglect and/or

verbal abuse is uncovered; physical abuse is more rare (approximately 2 percent of cases). Depending on the severity of what is uncovered, termination may be indicated. Parents should then notify the police and/or their local child abuse/neglect hot line.

Distress Signals from the Parent–Caregiver Relationship

"It was a rare situation where I really clicked with a nanny who didn't also click with my parents." This is how a mother described her childhood recollection of her own and her parents' relationship with several caregivers. This parent is referring to an important signal for parents to consider in their evaluation of the quality of care for their children. Some parents described a clack—some uneasy feeling about the caregiver beyond their understandable anxieties and conflicts as working parents (see Chapter 6). These were often ongoing struggles with caregivers who seemed to have personality problems, not just momentary irritability, low energy, or failure to perform a specific requested job function. The intense, interpersonal difficulty felt by parents in dealing with these caregivers was captured in the parents' labels for them. One mother referred to her caregiver as the "nanny Nazi," another, "Miss Perfect," still another, the "control freak." These charged descriptors suggest that there was some ongoing characterization of the caregiver as a problem, which, as is true in any interpersonal relationship, led to problematic exchanges. Not surprisingly, many of these parents reported feeling they were "walking on eggshells." In some cases, it was as if the emphasis had shifted away from the parent–caregiver relationship as a collaborative child care effort to handling the caregiver's ups and downs. Whether these situations reflect troubled caregivers, troubled parents, a resulting problematic parent–caregiver relationship, or simply a bad match may be difficult to sort out when things reach this point of disequilibrium. In such cases, ending the relationship may be the only option.

Conversely, parents feel a good match or click when there is a good-enough child care arrangement and relationship between their child and the caregiver. The relationship is a barometer to the care being provided. There are other ways to assess the care, such as the child's mood, or skill development, and the caregiver's way of managing the child's day and play activities. A child cannot tell a parent whether or not a caregiver is spending enough time interacting with him.

A more complicated situation arises when parents feel the arrangement is working for them—they focus more on their own needs than on the child's. This can lead to problems if the child's needs are not being met.

There is no way to predict which parent–caregiver relationships will work. There are, however, some powerful tools that parents have available to them to help ensure a good working arrangement: asking hard questions up front, careful monitoring early on, and ongoing attention to negotiating a collaborative relationship (see Chapters 6 and 7). Ultimately, if the child care arrangement isn't working for the parents, then it will not work for the child either.

THE UNPLANNED TERMINATION

"I think most of the problems that arise are between the parents and the caregiver and not the caregiver and the child." This was one mother's sense of what makes for difficulties in child care arrangements. Unplanned endings, abrupt endings to the parent–caregiver relationship, typically arise around surface crises that reflect underlying problems that had gone unattended. Parents report, in retrospect, some awareness that they had let things slide.

They describe ignoring internal signals of distress—worries and annoyances that fester until a crisis situation arises. Some seemingly small disagreement then precipitates the caregiver's dismissal.

These distress signals from the relationship were, for many parents, too weak or too conflictual to be noticed, except in passing. They were not consciously addressed or discussed openly between the parents themselves and between the parents and the caregiver. Such awareness and communication might have cleared the air or even strengthened their relationship.

Letting Things Slide: Nancy, a Mother, Struggles with Guilty Feelings

Nancy, a psychiatrist and mother of two children, provides an example of one of these signals going unattended. Nancy and her husband had decided that after their three baby-sitters, they wanted an au pair. "We thought it was better this way because we knew from the very beginning exactly when she would be leaving." The apparent reason for Nancy's concern sprang from the very first caregiver, Yvette, hired after her oldest child's birth. Yvette had been with them for nearly two years. When Yvette's own pregnancy encountered complications, she had to be bedridden. Nancy hired a temporary replacement. When Yvette miscarried a few weeks later, she asked for her job back. Nancy told us: "I felt very awkward. The other woman, who was working out very well, was in the house. I didn't know what to do. Then Tommy went to the door, opened it and said, 'Bye, bye, Yvette!' That settled it for me. He wanted her to leave so I was able to tell her she had to go."

Upon further discussion, Nancy revealed that she had been uneasy for some time with Yvette's performance. She felt concerned that Yvette was not able to offer Tommy enough stimulation now that he was becoming a toddler.

"She was fine when she could carry him around and bring him with her to watch her soaps, but I felt he needed more now that he had become more active." Nancy recounted that her neighbor had told her that she noticed Tommy seemed much happier with the new woman because she did more with him.

Nancy could not heed the internal signal of unease she had been feeling. What prevented her from doing so was her strong feeling of guilt that accompanied her concern for Yvette. Her guilt was too great for her to fire Yvette, especially when Yvette was having such difficulties with her pregnancy. Indeed, she was feeling too guilty even to allow herself to recognize that this was her wish. Nancy, a woman dedicated to a helping profession, simply could not allow herself to even think of firing Yvette!

Nancy's mind played tricks on her. Given how bad she was feeling for this woman who had just miscarried, Nancy could not follow what her own best judgment told her was in her son's best interest. But once she heard Tommy, she concluded that he did not want Yvette to stay; only then could she fire her.

At the end of the interview, we suggested to Nancy that perhaps Tommy's gesture might have had a different meaning than the one she understood it to have. Maybe she had to hear it this way because of her guilt feelings. Tommy might have been playing an age-appropriate game of peekaboo when he was opening the door for Yvette. It might be his way of trying to master the sudden disappearance and reappearance of someone who had been an integral part of his entire life thus far. Nancy then realized that she had to understand it the way she did because she would not have been able to fire Yvette otherwise. She was struggling with her own discomfort at disappointing Yvette.

We believe that Nancy might have been able to help Yvette and herself if she were able to listen to her internal signals.

She might have been able to plan a transition for Tommy
and help Yvette find another family with different needs.
And while Nancy felt that the youthfulness of the au pairs
would better suit both her toddler and her older, latency-
age child, her decision to use au pairs was motivated, in
part, by her wish to avoid any feelings of guilt in the future.

To Leave in Anger: The Emotional Wrestling
Match Between Maris, a Caregiver,
and Sarah, a Mother

Recall here the story of Maris, a full-time caregiver, who
told us of the unplanned termination that ended painfully
for everyone (see Chapter 3). She had been fired abruptly
following a series of struggles in her relationship with Sarah, mother of Sammy, a 5-year-old. Maris had helped bring
up Sammy since his birth. The day before the interview,
Maris had received a phone call from Sarah. Sarah said she
did not want Maris to speak to Sammy when Maris saw
him in the local playground (where she now spent time
taking care of another child).

Things came to a head when Sarah learned from a friend
that Maris had started to take college courses at night. The
eruption came when Maris was asked unexpectedly to stay
late on a night she had class. Maris recounted the interaction with Sarah: "She just disrespected me and told me I
had better do it. She called me a bitch and I said the same
and she just told me to get out now!" Maris was distraught
and angry as she spoke. Several months and several
caregivers later, Sarah had apparently mentioned to her
friends (who, in turn, mentioned to their caregivers) that
she would consider taking Maris back. Maris told us this
with a sense of pride, mingled with resentment for having
been so badly treated. There was also an air of reconcilia-
tion in Maris's tone: "If she approached me directly, I would
try to talk, but I'm too proud to beg."

This vignette captures the inherent conflicts over power, dependency, and the need for control that often underlie the relationship between parents and caregivers. Both Sarah's and Maris's inability to attend to their internal signals that things were amiss between them led to the moment of crisis and abrupt dismissal, which was not in Sammy's best interest.

The crisis that precipitated the end of their working relationship (and the care of Sammy, now in kindergarten) was Maris's desire to return to school. It was striking that Sammy had just started his school career as well. It was as if both mother and caregiver knew, at some level, that a transition and an inevitable loss were coming. They were, however, unable to focus on this reality in a direct way so that an optimal separation could be negotiated by all concerned. While the "fight" was ostensibly between Maris and Sarah, each feeling a loss of support from the other, the meaning of this loss went unnoticed and unexpressed by both. Sarah seemed incapable of acknowledging Maris's (and perhaps Sammy's) need to move on, to develop her own life. And Maris, for her part, felt her new independence with the advent of Sammy's move to a full-time school schedule should allow for her own personal development. Both these feelings are not unlike what many stay-at-home mothers feel once their children become less dependent. Not surprisingly, the ending was abrupt, negated and discounted rather than dealt with more directly. Hence the necessary mourning could not take place. As a result, Sammy's loss went unnoticed.

"I Can't Move On If I Don't Know Where I've Been": Christopher, a 7-Year-Old, Asks for Help in Mourning His Lost Caregiver

Christopher provides yet another example of the impact of unplanned departures on children. He angrily told his father, David, of his displeasure with his new caregiver, Molly: "She's not Laura!" Laura was the caregiver who had recently been fired due to her chronic lateness in the morning. Christopher felt attached to her and he liked her. Too young to understand the reasons for the dismissal, or to care, he clung to the memory of his lost beloved nanny. Whatever this new caregiver did, Christopher compared it to how Laura would have done it. The new caregiver always came up short. Christopher felt his loss painfully. In an effort to help his son, David responded to his son's complaint: "Right! I told you that you couldn't replace one person with another. They're simply not the same. People are different and you have to accept a person the way he or she is!"

This might seem to be a helpful comment to make. Indeed, people are different. But however well intentioned, Christopher's father had missed the point. Fortunately, his son had the capacity to form an attachment to Laura, even though she had been one of several caregivers. He knew all too well that they were not interchangeable! His protestation revealed that Laura was a distinct person to him, someone he preferred. Helpless to bring her back, Christopher could at least make it clear that he did not want this new person around. In part, this was a way for him to cope with his feelings of impotence in a decision that greatly affected his life, and in part he was trying to keep Laura alive within himself. Had his father been able to convey to him an understanding of his sense of loss, of the justifiable sadness and anger he felt at her leaving, of his frustration at not having any say in the matter, David would have fulfilled a very significant parental task for his son. He would have helped his son accept the loss as an inevitable part of life. This process, in turn, provides the foundation for accepting the inevitability of death, a lifelong task.

THE PLANNED TERMINATION

"At some point there's going to be a separation. I don't know how we're going to part. That's going to be a real difficult thing. I get afraid. Will her life fall apart? But for her to have had the stability and loving care that she's had makes up for the pain that will come when she has to separate. Because that's life." This is how a mother anticipated her child's feelings of loss of the caregiver (as well as her own relationship with the caregiver).

In their book *The Preschool Years: Family Strategies That Work—From Experts and Parents*, Ellen Galinsky and Judy David,[7] note that good endings to child care arrangements are those that allow for preparation. What has been found to be to the child's advantage is a termination that has been mutually agreed upon, planned for, and considered from the beginning of the relationship.

Even planned endings, while optimal, are still inherently stressful for all concerned. But, as we have noted, active acknowledgment of the feelings of loss offers the best chance for a good adaptation to loss and transition, a central, painful, yet potentially growth enhancing moment of life.

When possible, parents and caregivers together should set a realistic date to end their present arrangement. This affords an opportunity for everyone to prepare. It is helpful to create a realistic time frame for ending, one that will allow the necessary time for the emotional work every ending involves. Usually four to six months allows such a process to unfold. The process should begin with just the parents and caregivers; the children should not be involved. Parents should be a "container" for all of the issues and emotions that exist between them and the caregiver before addressing the reality of the transition with the children. Young children have no conception of time beyond the length of a Barney episode. The development of an adult sense of time occurs very gradually, starting around the age of 7 or 8.

The concept that the caregiver is leaving is an incomprehensible notion for a young child. In addition, if parents feel guilt and anxiety about the imminent departure, the children pick up on these emotions and become upset themselves, sensing that something is terribly wrong in their world.

Before addressing the termination with the children, the parents and caregiver need to talk together, to review their relationship and the feelings involved. When the timing of an ending is set unrealistically, such feelings are avoided or denied. If the parents themselves do not speak of their feelings, the child will be robbed of the chance to learn to deal fully with his or her own feelings, which is an essential part of life. Loss, separation, and death engender these types of feelings.

Care must be taken to meet everyone's needs when the present arrangement ends. What will the child, the parents, and the caregiver require when this present arrangement is over? Alternate arrangements to suit the growing child are essential. Parents need to be sure that their children will have what they need for their safety and growth. Caregivers must have a chance to secure their next job, especially if they are the sole provider for themselves and their families. All these arrangements take time to make, so that everyone's peace of mind is taken into account.

Helping Children Make the Transition

Young children may feel responsible for the abrupt changes in their world, such as when a caregiver is terminated. Adults may know that nothing they did or failed to do was involved, but we should never assume that children know this reality. When explanations for the ending of a caregiver's employment are offered to children, the focus should be on how this event is not their responsibility, but rather due to a change in the parents', caregiver's, or child's schedule, or an impending move.[8]

Infants and toddlers, and to some degree even older preschoolers, do not have the capacity to verbalize their feelings of confusion, anxiety, loss, or anger when the caregiver relationship ends. They are much more likely to express their distress through a variety of general stress reactions, which vary according to a child's developmental level.[9] For example, an infant may show little or no awareness of changes in caregivers. Toward the end of the first year and in the toddler phase as well, there may be increased fussing or temper tantrums. A young preschooler may become more aggressive with his play. He may break, take, or hide the favorite toy of a peer. Older preschoolers and school-age children may regress in their toileting or have nightmares. More verbal children may repeatedly ask questions about the caregiver's whereabouts. The absence of any obvious reaction should not lead parents to think that their child is having no reaction. Children are creatures of habit. They become attached to routines and to those who care for them. If there is a single recommendation we can make to parents about the ending phase of the caregiver relationship, it is to be mindful of the effect the loss is having on their children. Children need help in identifying what they feel—their sense of loss, sadness, anxieties, fears, and anger. Parents must create the space for them to know that these feelings are OK to have and to speak about. Then they will be better able to integrate the loss into their emotional lives.

The child's age should also set the boundaries for the information provided about the circumstances of the caregiver's termination.[10] Children only need to know and are only capable of using what they are capable of understanding (not what the parent may want to tell them for their own personal reasons). Such facts should be offered broadly and couched gently. For example, children need to know that while the caregiver will no longer be working with the family, she will still continue to love them and care about them. Even toddlers, although not yet verbal, need explanations they are capable of understanding. The parent's tone—calm, reassuring, and without blame—in communicating this news is important. Parents also must work through their own feelings with the caregiver. In abrupt, unplanned terminations, the pressure may be great to just get out the news. But here too, even a few hours or a day to put the situation in perspective and put oneself in the child's place can be invaluable. If a caregiver has left in anger (as in the case of Maris), and if the argument had been overheard by the child (as in the case of Tira), it is important to acknowledge that there was an argument, but that it was between the parent and the caregiver.

People often use familiar objects and rituals as emotional ballast when faced with life's inevitable changes. D. W. Winnicott first described this use of the familiar in times of change as "transitional phenomena."[11] He noted that children gravitate toward familiar and special objects and rituals to which they are attached, such as a favorite teddy bear, blanket, or song, as a way of managing anxieties around separation, loss, and the bittersweet feelings that come when they become more independent.

In a sense, we never completely grow out of the need for these comforting objects and experiences, but rather they become part of us and how we adapt to life's emotional challenges.[12] Objects such as mementos of pivotal occasions, pictures, songs, aromas, and familiar rituals are all part of the ways we learn to cope with change and soothe ourselves. When we leave a job or move, we often say, "We'll keep in touch" or "We'll see each other soon!" On one level, we do this to ease the pain that comes with separation and loss. On another level, we need to believe that nothing will change.

For children, the boundary between the wish that things can continue exactly as they had been and the fact that something is changing is not so clear. Holding onto a piece of the past, while moving into the future, is an important developmental step that is worked out gradually and evolves in new ways over time.

Children's attachments to their transitional objects demonstrate this emotional process of separating, at their own internal pace, from their need for the adults who care for them, while maintaining an internal emotional connection in their absence.

Here are some suggestions that can help children (and parents) during this transition:

- having a party, dinner, or special outing with the caregiver to mark the occasion, complete with pictures and mementos;
- having the child give a gift to the caregiver;
- reviewing old pictures of the child's time with the caregiver and adding current ones to a photo album or picture collage;
- reading animal stories about attachment and separation.

Even with younger children, there is a need to address this loss and this time of transition. Try to verbalize what you suspect they are feeling when you observe their play or their behavior, particularly in transitional times. For example, be sensitive to their routines with the caregiver, or when the caregiver would typically come and go. Talk to them about the caregiver's leaving. Even younger children will hear your emotional response, and your calming influence will create an atmosphere that gives them permission to have their own reactions and make the transition.

It can be extremely helpful, if the situation allows, for the old and new caregivers to overlap for a period of days.

This will help in providing a continuation of important routines. Also, acknowledging changes and seeing them occur helps children anticipate what lies ahead.

A good rapport between the old and new caregiver is particularly important, almost as much as a good parting between the old caregiver and the parents. If children feel that the adults in their world can tolerate difficult transitions with a sense of calm and a range of emotional reactions, this will do much to prevent loyalty tugs that children may feel when the important persons in their lives are at odds. As always, expect a stormy period. Try to minimize other changes in the child's life at this transitional time.

Working Out Loss and Making the Transition in Play: Mimi, a 4-Year-Old, Plays the "New Nanny Name Game"

Mimi, a bright 4-year-old girl, was actively dealing with the loss of her caregiver, Nina, who had been in her home since Mimi was a year old. The end came for this relationship when Nina decided to return to school full time, making it impossible for her to maintain even a part-time schedule with the family. Mimi's parents and the caregiver had begun, among themselves, and out of Mimi's awareness, to address this inevitable termination several months in advance. The separation process was ongoing and amicable. Both Mimi's parents and her caregiver were actively helping Mimi to make the transition by containing this process until they had worked it through in terms of their own feelings. They decided that Mimi should be told only a month or so before the transition, after they had ironed out all the details.

When they finally told Mimi, she became clinging and irritable. She wanted Nina to stay. She became defiant about the new caregiver, whom she would soon meet. But once allowed the space to do so, and once reassured by Nina that she would not forget about her, Mimi was able to make her own transition.

Mimi met with the new caregiver for a few brief periods during Nina's last week. She seemed to be actively working out the transition to the new caregiver, Nives, in a spelling game of her own making. Her happy and playful mood seemed to reflect both good memories of Nina, who was still alive for her, and some understandable anxiety about the new caregiver, Nives:

> Daddy, how do you spell "Nina"?
> [Father spells for her—N, I, N, A]
> Oh . . . Nina. N, I, N, A. And Daddy, how do you spell "Nives"?
> [Father spells for her—N, I, V, E, S]
> Oh . . . Nives. N, I, V, E, S. Nina, Nina, Niva, Niva, Niva, Nives. N, I, V, E, S. Nives! I have a new babysitter . . . N, I, V, E, S!

With this simple, yet poignant, word game, and with the help of her father who was able to engage her in this crucial play, little Mimi was finding a way to adapt to a painful loss. She could make the transition to a new caregiver and successfully become attached to her over time.

Letting Go by Holding Onto a Cherished Piece of the Past: The Parents' Work

Many parents also described their own struggles in terminating relationships with their children's caregivers, especially in cases where the caregiver had been part of their expanded familial space for a long time. How they deal with this transition is central to the child's ability to work through this transitional time, as we have seen in Mimi's story. Here's how a mother characterized her struggle to end a relationship with Sudha, her child's caregiver of six

years: "I think of her as a kindly old aunt . . . so much so
that it got to the point that there was no way to get rid of
or even think about getting rid of her because of certain
problems. I mean, how do you fire a kindly old aunt?"

Once she really acknowledged the strength of her familial connection with Sudha, it became easier to see the
difficulties that had evolved over time with her as an employee. Sudha had been a good-enough early child care
provider. But she was struggling with her own issues
around separation from the children in her charge, as well
as an ongoing difficulty with growing with the job.

The mother described the termination process, once begun, as an enormous relief to her and the caregiver. It
started with the caregiver's request for several weeks off
in order to visit family in India. While this was a rare request, it brought up a familiar pang of panic and then irritation (with the caregiver) for the mother: "I knew it was
about much more than the vacation request." She was able
to find temporary help during the vacation, and she began
to think about her hesitancy to address the lack of fit between her child care needs and what Sudha could provide.
With self-reflection and discussion with friends and family, she was able to connect this hesitancy to her own family history and the need for consistency for her children. She
realized that this need for consistency was no longer such
an issue since her son was older and she herself felt more
secure as a mother to her new baby. But still, this was a
loss. She therefore struggled to initiate an ending to the
relationship that she knew intuitively would be difficult for
all to manage.

The strength of the bond between mother, caregiver, and
the children was clear. Mother noted her initial hiring criteria and her sense of an ongoing connection, almost in the
same breath: "I was looking for continuity of care for my
kids. That was the most important part. I can't imagine

not seeing her from time to time and I would never deprive
the kids of that contact, either." Mother had also found her
own way to make the transition to a new caregiver and to
deal with the loss that this transition entailed. It was a
deeply personal expression of this mother's (and child's)
attachment to the caregiver, Sudha, and their attempt to
keep her with them by adopting a familiar part of her day-
to-day routine as their own.

When interviewed in her home, mother noted, in passing, that she was making bread in her new bread machine.
She loved the aroma and how secure it made her feel. It
was striking that, in the interviews, both mother and
caregiver had made reference to the "roti," the Indian bread
that the caregiver, Sudha, had made each day (see Chapter 4). We asked when did the new bread machine and the
bread making become part of the daily routine. She said
"Just after Sudha left."

Ties That Bind: A Year in the Life of a Child Can Feel Like a Lifetime

With au pairs, endings are arranged at the outset. But even
with these planned terminations, struggles with the degree
of attachment can complicate the endings.

Fatima, a young Moroccan woman, had come to New
York as an au pair with the idea of going to college. The
oldest daughter in a family of six children, she felt she was
a natural at child care. She decided to use this skill to gain
entry to what she hoped would be a world of greater opportunity, given her background of relative poverty (although middle class by Moroccan standards). Via an
agency, she was assigned to a family with an infant son,
Mark, and his older brother, Justin, who was just enter-
ing kindergarten.

At first it seemed a perfect arrangement. She would live
in and have her own separate wing of the large apartment.

The friendly and well-educated parents seemed encouraging of her plan to work for a year and then to pursue her own education if her work status could be attained through immigration. But this accepting atmosphere was quickly marred by Justin's reaction to the dark-complexioned Fatima. He was quiet and circumspect at first, which Fatima wrote off to the transition involved in accepting a new caregiver. She noted, "Then everything went to hell."

Justin vacillated between this stony silence and stubborn refusal, verbal tirades, and physical tantrums. He would scream repeatedly, "Go away, you darkie." Fatima felt moral outrage mingled with abject fear. "I was all settled in and had no choice but to try to make it work." She worked for days to address his "racist" comments but felt continually puzzled. "How could such a young child be so hateful and racist? It didn't make sense." She tried explaining that people came in all shades and that "skin was skin." A talk with the parents left things even more unsettled. They were indifferent at best. "He's just a kid—he'll grow out of it."

It occurred to Fatima at this point that perhaps this "racism" had something to do with his anger at his previous caregiver, a young, white au pair, a French girl named René. She noted, "he was focusing on the difference between us, the only one he could see." She attempted to talk to the parents about this hypothesis, but to no avail. They insisted that René was only a backdrop in his life, and that "he knows who his parents are."

Fatima dealt with this situation by taking a paradoxical approach. She told Justin that he could hate her if he wanted and that she hated what he was saying to her, but all this was his loss. "I had something fun to offer him. I can sing and play piano and roller-skate. I told him he could either join me or hate me because I was darker than him." She noted that it took a few weeks, but that Justin came around eventually. "When my year was almost up, I decided to return home. I was exhausted by this job."

Fatima had prepared him for a transition via discussions about her country and the trip to nearby France his family was planning in the next year that might bring a reunion with René. Justin made her a card on her last day. It read: "You are a good babysitter. I love you. Always. Justin."

Fatima's astute realization that Justin's anger at her had come from another place—his anger at René—was crucial not only to her survival in this position, but also in helping Justin cope with his loss. This realization allowed her to be herself, available to him in the present, rather than to withdraw emotionally from Justin out of anger toward him. The initial reaction of his parents to Fatima's connection of the "racism" to his anger at the loss of René suggested that they may have had their own difficulties with their loss of her. René had become part of the family and a "trusted source of support," as the mother had described in our separate interview with her. Their ambivalence was clearly noted in the stark contrast between their spoken (or unspoken) communication and their actions. Fatima said, "I never heard them mention René. Then suddenly, six months after I started, they flew to Paris for vacation (without the children) and planned to see her there."

In this case, despite the built-in termination posed by the selection of au pairs by these parents, there was an attachment to these women. This connection remained alive for them as noted in their continued contact with the au pairs from the past. Justin captured this unspoken connection and attachment in his latching onto the only obvious difference he could note between René and Fatima—skin color. His reaction also was a self-protective, defensive posture seen in many young children who lose someone close—

angry resistance to attaching again to a new caregiver. Despite the conscious attempt to build in a boundary for their attachment (i.e., a known termination point and a relative air of detachment), there was an unconscious and relatively enduring feeling about René, which remained unspoken.

The Ongoing Separation Process

Everyone has a characteristic style of coping with endings. Some people quarrel, as was the case with Tira, a caregiver (see Chapter 5) as well as Maris and Sara (above). People who have conducted in-service programs for in-home caregivers have also described this common pattern between parents and caregivers (which the children also adopted) who were ending their arrangements. "It was amazing!" the instructor told us. "They always pick a fight with one another. I say to myself, 'Yep, they're leaving, alright. Here's the usual fight that happens just before they do.'" In contrast, some people devalue the other, saying to themselves, "Who cares? I don't need her anyway! She didn't really mean that much to me. I can live without her." Others approach this issue by simply avoiding it altogether. They allow an arrangement to continue long past its usefulness. They simply can't end.

Without an awareness of how to approach separation, the parents' behavior gives a powerful lesson to their child. Parents should ask themselves, "Is this the lesson I wish my child to learn? Is this the way I would like my child to take leave of me?"

Even when care is taken for a planned termination, inevitably anxieties arise. For example, parents expressed concern to us about their caregiver's capacity to continue to look after their children with the same level of attention and dedication once a termination date had been settled upon: "Would she leave emotionally before leaving physically?" Besides expressing a concern for their child's continued well-being, this worry revealed a common struggle: Who shall be left by whom, and who will leave first before being left? When a necessary ending is not planned and dealt with, the press for termination will show up in one way or another. One father dealt with it this way: "She wants another raise? That's it! We're getting rid of her." Thus ended a four-year relationship with their caregiver.

A Mother and Caregiver Struggle to Move On

One mother, Peggy, provides another example of the difficulty of moving on. She had Nora, her child's caregiver, for over ten years. Although the relationship had its difficulties, by everyone's assessment it had been a successful one. Each had come to know the other's expectations and limitations. Each knew how to manage well enough with the other so that there existed a reservoir of mutual good will between them created over these many years together. This was something they both drew upon when inevitable tensions arose, and arise they did! The following provides one such example:

> My family and I returned home from vacation late Saturday night to find nothing at all to eat. We were tired and hungry. I felt furious! Nora had been paid as usual for the week, but she had done nothing at all in the house, not even make sure we had something to eat! She thinks she was on vacation!
>
> Just because we're on vacation doesn't mean she is. I told my husband that when she comes in on Monday morning, that's it! She's had it! She's through! Does she think I'm a jerk? The least she could have done was stock the fridge. Nothing! Nada!

Peggy was lucky in having a husband with whom she could "vent." She said that after she had gotten her anger out of her system, she realized that she could not possibly fire Nora like that.

> I was using this as an excuse, a justification, for ending with her. I guess I have to face the fact that we just don't need her the way we did. My children are old enough now to come home alone. But I'm having a hard time just letting her go. I feel guilty. It's not like she's just an employee. She is, but she's more than that. She's become part of the family, so much so that she feels that when we're on vacation, so is she! Sometimes I wish we had just had one of those relationships where people feel OK with just saying: "Thank you very much, but we no longer need your services." But I'm a softee. Will she be able to get another job, given her age now? I worry. This is not doing me any good because I know I have to let her go but I'm having a hard time getting myself to do it. Then what happens is I feel like firing her when something like this happens.

Peggy was right. She knew she had a justifiable reason to fire Nora. She felt used, taken advantage of, and inconvenienced. Yet she also knew that she ought not terminate the relationship out of pique. The real reason Peggy had to terminate their arrangement was because there was no longer a need for a full-time caregiver in her and her children's lives. Nora had been very important for all of them. Nora and Peggy both had to face the ongoing paradox at the heart of their relationship. She was not a member of the family, after all, and since her reason for being employed no longer existed, her status as employee was very much in question.

We might understand that, in addition to Nora's provocative behavior during that vacation week, Peggy's anger was also a reaction to not wanting to face the fact that it was time to end. She wished Nora would just leave, recognizing that she was no longer needed.

I know I'm the one who has to do it. But it's not easy. I
feel so heartless. I don't know if she'll be able to find another job—she's a lot older now. People at work get laid
off all the time, especially in this age of downsizing. But
somehow this feels different. Why? Why is it so tough? And
why do I care so much? I keep reminding myself that she
is, after all, an employee.

Yes, but not just an employee. This is precisely why it
is so difficult to alter the arrangement and let Nora go,
especially when she faces limited options. When family
members part ways, irrevocably, it is usually because of
bitter feelings unresolved between them. Otherwise, family relationships don't "end." They shift and change. Only
death ends them, and that is no simple matter either. The
relationship between caregivers and parents (and, in different and complex ways, for the children) is different. Their
contact began and continued out of mutual, although different, needs. When those needs are no longer mutual, the
relationship becomes strained for one or both parties. When
it's over, it's over. Peggy was struggling to face the inevitable. She knew that she wanted to plan for their parting
in a way that would take into account Nora's need for some
transition time as well as her family's need to replace her
with a part-time housekeeper, something Nora could not
afford to consider.

Ultimately, Peggy had a choice in how this termination
would unfold. She did several simple things following her
return from vacation. First, she stopped. We strongly rec-
ommend this crucial first step. Peggy did not pick up the
phone that Saturday night and tell Nora off, as she felt like
doing, because this is very complicated and loaded with
feelings. There are clues that should tell us precisely when
we should stop—feeling like jumping out of your skin, your
heart pounding, feeling like screaming, scolding, cursing.
It is best to stop, because once something is said, it cannot
be unsaid.

Second, Peggy stepped back. She ran through, in her mind, a variety of scenarios of what she could do when she saw Nora on Monday. These ran from the wild to the reasonable. She considered various ways to approach the immediate problem at hand as well as the larger issue of letting Nora go. She tried them out on her husband to get his input and feedback. This was trial thinking, trying various realistic approaches. She steadied herself by keeping her eye on the whole picture. She remembered the history that existed between them. Doing so enabled Peggy not to fire Nora in a ruthless way.

We might wonder what would lead Nora to behave as thoughtlessly as she had over the family's vacation. Had she acted out of envy toward the family, an envy that was so strong that the only way she could behave was to be on vacation herself, thereby lessening that envy? Was she, in her own way, forcing the unspoken issue of termination on Peggy by her provocative behavior? Was she looking for her employer to set limits with her? Was she looking to be fired? Was she having difficulty facing the facts herself? We offer the same recommendation to this caregiver that we offer to parents: stop, step back, and think. Tira, the caregiver in Chapter 5, might have acted differently had she followed these simple steps. Instead, she gave her notice in a huff, acting out of feelings of entitlement and resentment that had much more to do with her own family history and unmet needs than with her history with her employers. Indeed, Emily, the child in her care whom she loved, would have been given a better model to follow if both caregiver and parents had been able to manage their feelings at this tense moment.

It is easy to deny the impact that separation, even ones that are planned, have on children. One mother, Doris, had a caregiver for seven years. A suitable time had been agreed upon so that Doris could find another caregiver since the present caregiver had to return to her own country. Doris's older children, now 9 and 11, "don't really care or notice" that the caregiver was leaving, Doris assured herself. "It's harder for my 4-year-old," Doris told the interviewer. It is understandable that she would say this. She was in a near panic, having just found out that the replacement she had found had taken another job the very day she was to begin. Desperate to find someone suitable and pressed for time, Doris could not even notice that her children, who had known the caregiver almost all their lives, would have feelings about her going, especially given the likelihood that they would never see her again. The sense of urgency about finding someone to care for the children so that she would not neglect her work, coupled with the strong wish she had to be certain that she did not settle for just anyone, made the situation more tense for everyone. Speaking of the woman she thought she had hired, Doris told me that she had some clues that something might happen like this. "I just didn't want to think about it. She seemed like such a good caregiver and I was desperate. She told me she was also looking at another job, but it just didn't register. Now look where I am!"

This was a frequent refrain we heard. When pressured by time constraints, parents tended to overlook what they didn't want to see. It was suggested to Doris that perhaps she should give herself some leeway by finding someone she might use temporarily. "I did find someone else we all liked very much but she didn't want to live in. Maybe I could use her until we find someone that could fit the bill for us," Doris said in a relieved voice. It helps to find a way out of the tremendous temporary pressures so that choosing the proper caregiver will not take second place. This burdened mother might also then be able to attend to the very important parental task of teaching her children how to deal with loss.

It's About Time, It's About Space: The Many Meanings of Money at Termination

Many parents, particularly those whose relationship with their caregiver spanned years rather than months, described an intricate dance of extreme shifts along the continuum when the formal ending to their relationship drew near. At one moment, they seemed to characterize the relationship as strictly employer–employee and at the other extreme, like "members of the family." These shifts occurred as they attempted to deal with the real issues that arise and the disequilibrium that results when child care responsibilities change. This loss of the as-if quality of the relationship typically occurs when children begin preschool or kindergarten. Hours change, responsibilities shift, and the emotional issues surface. The fact that the caregiver may feel entitled to some breathing space and monetary reward for her tenure during this transitional time often puts parents squarely in touch with their ambivalent attachment to the caregiver. As a result, parents may feel entrapped by their own attachment to the caregiver.

Sweet Sorrow: Amy and Richard Negotiate Their Ending with Rose, a Caregiver

Here's how one mother, Amy, and father, Richard, described the process of separating from their daughter Carlie's caregiver, Rose, after four years of employment. They had been giving Rose annual raises, and saw themselves as good employers, particularly now that their daughter Carlie was in preschool. Together with Rose, they had slipped into a new arrangement, with only minimum discussion of the details. While she was receiving the same pay, Rose agreed to spend part of her day doing more cooking and light housekeeping. The actual hours of hands-on care for Carlie had been reduced. Amy described her emotional juggling act:

I felt like it was healthier for me not to know what time she got here each day. I just knew she was doing the work that we asked. I knew I would resent it if I knew for sure that I was paying her for more hours than she used to work. At work, my employees come in at 10 and leave at 6. But with Rose, I can either make myself nuts and wonder what time she gets there, or let it go.

Amy's hopes and expectations, previously out of her awareness, seemed to bubble up as she talked more about her struggle to make sense out of the push and pull of this transitional time.

My hope would be that she would be there if I needed her—like if Carlie got sick after I dropped her at school and she needed to come home. On the other hand, it doesn't exactly make sense to have her sitting there all morning waiting for a call that usually won't come. I mean she's always there if I can't take Carlie to school, or on half days or school vacations. She doesn't need the entire day to cook and clean until it's time to pick up Carlie.

Richard put it this way:

It's a transitional time. We thought about letting her go sooner, but we decided to "bite the bullet." She has a strong relationship with Carlie, and vice versa. I guess it's like an insurance policy, knowing she's around. When everything is going fine, you don't think about it. You don't need it. Even though she's not working the same number of hours, I guess she's earned it—a little leisure—her "equity" maybe! At the beginning, when Carlie as born, she worked 10-hour days sometimes. Her pay was lower than it is now. And now, she's making much more per hour since she's probably working fewer hours.

Amy and Richard felt they were being more than generous with Rose. When it came up in conversation that Rose had heard about a woman who worked at home and needed

a few hours' coverage in the mornings, Amy *told herself*
"Great . . . she's starting to figure out what her next gig
might be—to work for someone else in the morning and for
us in the afternoons." But Rose had something else in mind.
She told Amy that she assumed they would still keep her
on full salary, a retainer, because she would still be available for Carlie as much as they needed her. Amy "blew up"
at Rose:

> I said to Rose, "You're only with Carlie in the afternoon
> and there is less to do. How could you imagine we would
> pay you for the mornings that you worked for someone
> else?" She yelled back, "There is more to do—now I'm do-
> ing cooking and cleaning." We just ended it there. I know
> I felt resentment, like an employer who had been cheated.
> It's like an employee double dipping. Later I told her I felt
> very strongly that I shouldn't pay her for hours that she
> works for another family. It's just so illogical. I can't be-
> lieve that she expected to be paid for those hours she was
> away from us.

Rose's thought of double dipping was, as an employee,
unreasonable and illogical. On the other hand, this expectation seemed a direct corollary to Amy and Richard's unspoken expectation at other moments that she be available
simply out of her attachment to them and Carlie, not as a
valued employee but as a member of the family.

Amy and Richard were asked to explore some of these
intense feelings—beyond simply dismissing Rose's expectation as illogical. At times, money and pay had been a
struggle between these parents and caregiver, but somehow they had weathered many storms together. Richard
and Amy have complementary struggles around the inevitable process. Richard said, "It feels funny, this thought of
her working for another family. It's like, you know, she's
ours. Like part of our family. She works for us, but she's
our daughter's caregiver."

Amy had a slightly different take:

Well, it doesn't feel so funny to me—that is, I can understand it. She's always been a great nurturer—to Carlie and
to me, too—to us as parents as well. Maybe she needs to
care for an infant again. Then again, maybe that's my fan-
tasy. Maybe it's my own thing and I have my own issues
with my daughter growing up. Maybe she's relieved to be
free of the day-to-day grind of it. She does seem happier
with the schedule. I guess she has worked pretty darn hard
for us.

Then Richard chimed in:

Yup, I guess she has a right to a life, too. She worked for
years, 8 A.M. to 6 P.M. She's served her time and this is a
little bit of a reward. It's a little like the corporate world.
You start out with long hours, low on the totem pole. Ideally you move up, get promoted, and make more money,
have more freedom, don't punch a clock.

When parents identify their own feelings and then open
a nondefensive dialogue with the caregiver, a possibility
exists to arrive at an ending that best serves the interests
of all involved. In this case, these parents held widely conflicting views, not so much from each other but within
themselves. On the one hand, they were incredulous that
Rose thought she should be paid by them for the hours she
worked for another family. This seems reasonable. Yet, by
their own admission, it only speaks to the employee part
of the equation, where they were stuck at the moment.
They later agreed that Rose had earned the right to have
the greater flexibility she enjoyed. How long and within
what boundary had become the unspoken issue between
them.

From her perspective as a loyal employee, Rose agreed
with this notion. But her expectation that they pay her was
an extreme position, not unlike the expansion in her life

that a mother might feel after her children become more independent. It is ironic that the same currency was seen in such different ways. Things broke down when mother, father, and caregiver were not talking, but nursing their silent expectations, fears, and resentments. They may have ultimately arrived at this negotiated agreement to pay a salary for Rose's availability and new housework chores on her schedule and not "on demand." Such a negotiation would have undoubtedly brought up some of the underlying issues and feelings of attachment, dependency, and loss that are always swirling around these transitions and endings.

Amy's issues around separation and loss of this relationship with Rose emerged at the end of our interview. Having talked about her anger and ambivalence enabled her to be aware of her inevitable loss. Rose was not only her employee but someone who had become a core part of the extended familial space.

> I'm very nervous about letting go. She has been such a stable force—not only in Carlie's life but in our life. I'm not sure how ready I am to have that discussion. If it's not what she wants, then she'll be out of our lives, and that's a little daunting. Ideally, I'd like her to get a morning job and stay on for a few more years. But I don't know what her plans are. I guess we need to talk.

9

Why It Works
When It Does

In December 1997, archaeologists reported having found the tomb of the wet nurse of Tutankhamen, the boy pharaoh of ancient Egypt.[1] The memorial to a caregiver is an extremely rare instance of ancient Egyptians devoting an entire tomb to a woman. This finding confirms both the existence of caregivers in ancient times and the esteem in which they were held. We can assume it was a successful relationship, given such a tribute.

For some people, successful child care means someone is dependable, showing up when they should be, thereby making life easier. They feel their children are safe. To others, it is seeing their children loved by someone who tends to their physical and emotional needs as they grow. To still others, a successful caregiver stimulates the children's intellectual development as well as tends to their physical and emotional needs.

Successful child care hinges on the quality of the relationship parents establish with their caregiver. Over and over again in our interviews, we heard a similar refrain: this relationship works because there is a feeling of mutual respect for one another and a regard for one another's feelings and needs.

Demand for good child care far outweighs the supply. The White House conference on child care addressed what has been referred to as the "silent crisis." Few formal child care quality assurance programs are in place around the country. Criteria for licensing and accreditation policies vary greatly from state to state. Rosemarie Jordano, president of Children First, Inc., a national corporate child care backup system, and Marie Oates, director of Bayridge, a Boston center for university and professional women,[2] point out that the silent crisis has as much to do with ignorance and expectations as with a lack of consistent standards. As we have stated frequently throughout this book, there is a greater likelihood of success when parents and caregivers alike know what to expect from one another and what to demand of one another. Frequently, the disparity between the tremendous responsibility that caregivers assume and the salary they receive is one cause of discontent and turnover. We have seen, however, that more is involved in ameliorating this crisis than better salary and benefits, higher professionalism, and greater training, essential as these undoubtedly are.

These relationships endure when a feeling of respect for one another infuses the negotiations that take place in establishing job description, recompense, benefits, and schedule. Often these discussions are messy, fraught with intense feelings and the frustrations of limited energy, time, and money. When the mother can acknowledge that the caregiver is a working woman who, like herself, wants to be treated with respect, she creates rapport between them. Simply put, it is the old golden rule of doing unto others as you would have others do unto you.

In *Getting to Yes Without Giving In*, Bill Ury and Roger Fisher[3] suggest a strategy for successful negotiation that they have used in mediating peace talks in troubled countries throughout the world. They argue that positional bargaining—staking out a position, usually an extreme one to start with, then reluctantly narrowing the gap between what's asked and what's offered in a series of small painful steps—makes for bad feelings and worse deals. Instead they suggest what they call "principled negotiation": probing the other person's underlying, often unstated interests, then exploring how these overlap with one's own. Their main objective is to teach people to be curious, to look at things from a new perspective.

Wherever we found a successful parent–caregiver relationship, this curiosity existed. The parents wanted to know what their caregiver needed to feel comfortable, satisfied, and reassured. Often their motives for being curious were mixed—a blend of respect, fear of loss, resignation as well as concern for the caregiver. They sought the points of mutual, overlapping interest. This usually began with both parent and caregiver genuinely involved with the child's well-being, how each understood what the child needed at a given point. It proceeded with an acknowledgment of what each of them wished for from the other as well as for themselves. One father put it this way: "A caregiver also organizes you. She brought her cultural biases with her and some things she preferred to hear from me, the dad, rather than from my wife. There was no sense here of political correctness. The goal is to deal effectively enough that you can provide the best care for your child when you're away."

Every satisfied interviewee referred to an early feeling of clicking, a good fit, a match of temperaments with the caregiver. One mother put it this way: "If it works, you'll have this type of feeling; if it doesn't, you won't. If it's there, you're going to put up with more stuff than you would have imagined you would, and you will find yourself doing things you might never have imagined. For instance, I started looking for health insurance coverage for her family; I have friends who have bought cars for their nannies." Often such help given caregivers goes well beyond the agreement they have between them. But there is often a feeling of wanting to help, as if she were a member of the family.

Dora, an owner and administrator of a private hospital in the South, spoke of her children's caregiver with great affection. "She's been part of our family for thirty-five years. Whenever someone in the family gets married, Tessy walks down the aisle with the rest of us. She's been with me through every one of my children's births, schooling, and weddings. She is part of my family and we are committed to her." Her high school friend, whom she was visiting, coaxed her further: "Tell her about the beautiful hysterectomy you gave her!" Dora described the excellent care Tessy received at her hospital when she needed surgery. She was given a private room with private nurses, all gratis. "She got the same treatment anyone else in our family would have gotten. Like I said, she's one of us."

Two and a half years after our first interview with Georgia, a mother with a 2-year-old, we interviewed her again. By this second conversation, Georgia had had a second son, now 10 months old. She was still very satisfied with her caregiver, the same woman she has had from the start. Yet it was clear that the honeymoon was over. A second child had brought added responsibilities and stress to the caregiver arrangement, as it had to the rest of the family.

Our caregiver, Meg, is a functional part of our family. We have the same ups and downs as she does. She bought a house upstate where she hopes to retire, so we lent her our station wagon to help transport some of her stuff. When she needed extra money for the closing, we lent it to her—paid her early. She's an integral part of our family, not a separate entity that gets plugged in and out. This makes it somewhat burdensome because her problems become our problems. But we're willing to do this because I feel our kids are getting really good care so I'm willing to put up with a lot. My kids are healthy, reasonably well adjusted, secure. That makes it worth the effort it takes to include Meg in our family as we do.

In this second interview, Georgia did not feel the same excitement she had conveyed when we first met. The realities of daily life with a second child to care for and support, Meg's aging impacting on her capacity to care for the new baby—different from how she had cared for their first son, the financial burdens on the couple as well as added demands on their time with their new son, the wear and tear of day-to-day living and managing the multiple relationships involved—all this was part of the feeling Georgia conveyed that, while things were not great as she had felt at the first interview, they were quite definitely good enough.

Just as in a marriage, the relationship between parents and caregivers can go through a honeymoon before settling into living relatively comfortably together. Things change. Children's needs change developmentally. Life presents challenges and surprises—for the parents, the caregivers, and the children as well. Some are welcome, others have to be endured. Every marriage depends on how well these vicissitudes are managed together. So too in this relationship. Like a marriage, it has to be constantly worked at for it to succeed. It happens in a marriage that, at times, one party carries the well-being of the relationship more than the other. It may shift. But both parties have to want it to succeed and work toward that success. So, too, here. Yet the responsibility rests primarily on the parents to see to the success of this relationship between them and their caregiver.

In one household where the caregiver of ten years had gone from taking care of the children to becoming the housekeeper, the mother told us that she felt she could overlook and accept many shortcomings and difficulties in their relationship because Iris met her basic needs. "I trust her with the most important things in my life—my children, running the household, our meals. She's smart, competent, trustworthy, reliable. With these qualities I can accept the shortcomings she has." Over the years, this mother had worked to separate out unrealistic expectations from realistic ones. "I had longed for the perfect caregiver, the perfect fairy godmother, really. It didn't take long to realize Iris would never be that—nor could anyone, for that matter. Once I realized that, I could better accept the person she was and appreciate the basically good job she was doing for us."

The father of this household put it this way: "Iris gets things done and doesn't bother me. She knows how to please me and she isn't intrusive. When there's a problem, I let my wife deal with it. Iris reports to her. That's it." He viewed the relationship as employer–employee. Happily he had his wife to tend to those matters that related to Iris being like a member of the family. This division worked for this couple.

Stephen Covey's book, *The Seven Habits of Highly Effective Families*, applies his seven habits to strengthening the family. The habits can be used to describe positive aspects of the good relationships we saw among parents and caregivers. These were households in which parents were able to be proactive, to act rather than react. They made their expectations clear from the start and readjusted or refined them as circumstances changed. As Covey put it, they acted on values rather than reacting to circumstances or emotions of the moment. His concept of "emotional bank accounts," an emotional reservoir of things that build trust in the relationship and things that decrease that trust, is what we have referred to throughout the book as a capacity to hold onto the ongoingness of the relationship. It is this capacity to remember the positive experiences that the caregiver has provided for the children and the family that helps to sustain parents during the inevitable hard times and angry feelings. It is a capacity to tolerate ambivalence.

In "highly effective" families, needs and expectations are communicated on a regular basis. We found that the parent–caregiver relationships that worked best were those that had built into them, on the caregiver's paid time, an opportunity to go over the schedule and the events of the day. When problems arose, they could be handled together, given that this custom was already in place. The parents had to understand the caregiver's perspective before they could expect her to understand and cooperate with their expectations. That is the way success in this relationship can be built. As Covey points out, when people know they will have an opportunity to be heard, it builds a willingness to listen.

Every relationship, especially one that unfolds within the heart of the family, is bound to have its ups and downs. Throughout the book, we have pointed to trouble signals and warning signs. Stress, fatigue, overwork, pressures of time, and money can keep parents from attending to problems. In addition, intense feelings from the past, as we have seen, get interwoven with those of the present, feelings that inevitably arise in the care of children. Intense attachments to important people in our daily lives arise and affect behavior in both conscious and unconscious ways. The more awareness parents bring to what happens between them and their caregiver, the more likely they can be proactive, creating the circumstances they desire. Once again, success depends on their taking responsibility. There is a direct correlation between parents' capacity to be self-reflective, to notice their own shifting feelings and moods toward their caregiver, and the quality of the relationship between parents and caregivers.

We noted the excitement one mother, the director of a prestigious organization, had in speaking about her caregiver. It was a good match, and she felt her children were being well cared for. "It's because of her that I can be where I am. I always wanted to work and have a family. I can do it because I trust her. Somebody once said that behind every great man there's a woman. Well, behind every woman I think there's got to be a great caregiver! I'm very grateful to her."

A final story stands out as particularly poignant in our interviews. Sheila had an only son, Matt, who was sickly from birth. Bedridden, he needed constant care. She had had several caregivers until she found Agnes, a Polish immigrant who spoke little English but whose kindness and devotion were eloquent. She came to the family when the child was 3. It clicked from the start between the child and Agnes and between Agnes and Sheila. In time and because of Agnes's dependability, Sheila was able to travel to Romania to adopt a son. It was an arduous process that required her leaving Matt in Agnes's hands, confident that he was well cared for and loved. At the time of the interview, Sheila's adopted son was 4 years old. Matt had died two years earlier. "I would never have Mark if it were not for her," Sheila told me with tears in her eyes. "It was because I knew that Matt was in such good hands that I could make the two trips that took me from him. I knew she loved him and cared about him almost as much as if not as much as I did. She didn't do it for the money, although I paid her for the extra time it required of her. She really did it because she cared about him—and about me. She must have known, as I did, that Matt would not live long. When he died, she mourned as if it were her own son. It often felt like he was a son to her, too. How can that ever be repaid?"

The bond between these two women went far beyond the ordinary boundaries of employer–employee. Because of her loving care, Agnes gave Sheila the peace of mind to enable her to leave him for her journey to adopt another child. Without such assurance of quality care and attention,

Sheila would never have gone, and would probably never have found Mark. Agnes gave what could never be bought. Sheila will be forever grateful to her.

These two women, and so many others like them that we interviewed, had found a balance. They could move between the boundaries that were inevitable in this caregiver relationship, within the extended familial space, where maternal functions and attachments were shared and then relinquished every day. They could bear the harshness of life and its exquisite beauty—present in the development of every child, and in the course of every relationship that has any meaning. We know that these relationships do not always work out so ideally. Yet when they do, we have seen the best in human nature, reminding us that decency, dedication, generosity, respect, kindness, and constancy are not in short supply.

Endnotes

INTRODUCTION

1. In a recent count, there were hundreds of Websites for parents on finding, hiring, training, and managing their caregiver-employees.

2. Denise Buffa and Kate Sheehy, D. A. Rips Judge's 'Bizzare' Ruling. Grief or Relief Depends on Which Parents. *New York Post*, 11 November 1997, p. 2.

3. Debra Rosenberg, The Nanny Spin Wars. *Newsweek*, 17 November 1997, pp. 74–76.

4. Debra Rosenberg and Evan Thomas, I Didn't Do Anything. *Newsweek*, 10 November 1997, pp. 60–63.

5. Andrea Peyser, Killer Goes Free as Judge Ito, uh, Zobel Caves in to Fan-Club Justice. *New York Post*, 11 November 1997, p. 4.

6. Child Care and Working Parents, *Nightline*, ABC News, October 21, 1997.

7. Eric Schmitt, Crying Need; Day Care Quandary: A Nation at War with Itself. *New York Times*, 11 January 1998, sec. 4, pp. 1, 4.

8. Edward Shorter, *The Making of the Modern Family*. New York: Basic Books, 1977.

9. David Elkind, *The Ties That Stress*. Cambridge, MA: Harvard University Press, 1996.

10. Donald W. Winnicott, Transitional Objects and Transitional Phenomena. *International Journal of Psychoanalysis* 34(2):89–97, 1953.

11. Geraldine Youcha, *Minding the Children: Childcare in America from Colonial Times to the Present*. New York: Scribner, 1995.

12. Faye E. Dudden, *Serving Women: Household Service in Nineteenth Century America*. Middletown, CT: Wesleyan University Press, 1983.

13. *Webster's Seventh New Collegiate Dictionary*. Springfield, MA: G. & C. Merriam, 1970.

CHAPTER 1

1. Rosalind C. Barnett and Caryl Rivers, *She Works, He Works*. San Francisco: Harper, 1996.

2. U.S. Bureau of Labor Statistics, 1993.

3. Judith Stacey, *In the Name of the Family*. Boston: Beacon, 1996.

4. U.S. Census data, 1993.

5. Erna Furman, *Preschoolers: Questions and Answers. Psychoanalytic Consultations with Parents, Teachers, and Caregivers*. Madison, CT: International Universities Press, 1995.

6. Susan Kontos, *Family Day Care. Out of the Shadows and Into the Limelight*. Washington, DC: National Association for the Education of Young Children, 1992.

7. Beth Azar, Data Released from Child-Care Study. *The Monitor*, American Psychological Association, June 1995.

8. R. R. Ruopp and J. Travers, Janus Faces Day Care: Perspectives on Quality and Cost. In *Day Care: Scientific and Social Policy Issues*, ed. E. F. Zigler and E. W. Gordon, pp. 72–101. Boston: Auburn House, 1982.

9. Susan Kontos et al., *Quality in Family Child Care and Relative Care*. New York: Teachers' College Press, 1995.

10. National Association for the Education of Young Children. Washington, DC.

11. National Association for Family Child Care. Washington, DC.

12. Eric Schmitt, Crying Need; Day Care Quandary: A

Nation at War with Itself. *New York Times*, 11 January 1998, sec. 4, pp. 1, 4.

13. Sandra L. Hofferith, The Demand for and Supply of Child Care in the 1990's. In *Child Care in the 1990's; Trends and Consequences*, ed. Alan Booth, pp. 3–25. Hillsdale, NJ: Lawrence Erlbaum, 1992.

14. Erna Furman, *Preschoolers: Questions and Answers*, op. cit.

15. M. K. Nelson, Mothering Other's Children: The Experiences of Family Day Care Providers. In *Circles of Care: Work and Identity in Women's Lives*, ed. E. Abel and M. Nelson, pp. 210–232. Albany, NY: SUNY Press, 1991.

16. Margaret McKim, Quality Child Care: What Does it Mean for Individual Infants, Parents and Caregivers? *Early Childhood Development and Care* 88:23–30, 1993.

17. Sally Provence, Infant Day Care: Relationships Between Theory and Practice. In *Day Care: Scientific and Social Policy Issues*, ed. E. F. Zigler and E. W. Gordon, pp. 33–55. Boston: Auburn House, 1982.

18. Kontos, *Quality in Family Child Care and Relative Care*, op. cit.

19. Jonathan Gathhorne-Hardy, *The Unnatural History of the Nanny*. New York: Dial, 1972.

20. Faye E. Dudden, *Serving Women: Household Service in Nineteenth-Century America*. Middletown, CT: Wesleyan University Press, 1983.

21. Susan Tucker, *Telling Memories Among Southern Women: Domestic Workers and Their Employers in the Segregated South*. New York: Schocken, 1988.

22. Geraldine Youcha, *Minding the Children: Childcare in America from Colonial Times to the Present*. New York: Scribner's, 1995.

23. Julia Wrigley, *Other People's Children*. New York: Basic Books, 1995.

24. Susan Cheever, The Nanny Track. *New Yorker*, 6 March 1995.

25. Stacey Schiff, The Runaway Mother. *New Yorker*, 10 November 1997, pp. 78–83.

CHAPTER 2

1. Susan Chira, *A Mother's Place*. New York: Harper Collins, 1998.
2. Judith Stacey, *In the Name of the Family*. Boston: Beacon, 1996.
3. David Elkind, *The Ties That Stress: The New Family Imbalance*. Cambridge, MA: Harvard University Press, 1996.
4. David Elkind, *The Hurried Child: Growing Up Too Fast Too Soon*. Reading, MA: Addison Wesley, 1981.
5. Robert Coles, *The Well-Off and the Rich in America*. Boston: Little, Brown, 1977.
6. Janet Gonzalez Mena, *Multicultural Issues in Child Care*. Mountain View, CA: Mayfield, 1993.
7. David Matsumoto, *Culture and Psychology*. New York: Brooks/Cole, 1993.
8. Gary R. Weaver, The Crisis of Cross-Cultural Child and Youth Care. In *Choices in Caring: Contemporary Approaches to Child and Youth Care Work*, ed. M. A. Krueger and N. W. Powell, pp. 65–103. Washington, DC: Child Welfare League of America, 1990.
9. David Matsumoto, *Culture and Psychology*, op. cit.
10. Edward Hall, *Beyond Culture*. New York: Anchor, 1977.
11. Theodora Abel, Rhoda Metraux, and Samuel Roll, *Psychotherapy and Culture*. Albuquerque: University of New Mexico Press, 1987.
12. RoseMarie Perez Foster, Michael Moskowitz, and Rafael Art. Javier, eds., *Reaching Across Boundaries of Culture and Class*. Northvale, NJ: Jason Aronson, 1996.
13. M. H. Van Ijzendoorn and P. M. Kroonenberg, Cross-Cultural Patterns of Attachment: A Meta-Analysis of the Strange Situation. *Child Development* 59:147–156, 1988.
14. Matsumoto, *Culture and Psychology*, op. cit.
15. Jean S. Phinney, When We Talk About American Ethnic Groups, What Do We Mean? *American Psychologist* 51(9):918–927, 1996.
16. Geraldine Youcha, *Minding the Children*. New York: Scribner's, 1995.

17. A. Prost and G. Vincent, *A History of Private Life: Riddles of Identity in Modern Times*. Cambridge, MA: Harvard University Press, 1991.

18. Shari Thurer, *Myths of Motherhood*. New York: Viking Penguin, 1994.

19. Hilary Waldman, Support for New Mothers, Thy Name is 'Doula.' *Hartford Courant*, 1 May 1997, p. A1.

20. Julia Wrigley, *Other People's Children*. New York: Basic Books, 1995.

21. Robert Hanley, Edison Couple Held in Death of Nanny. *New York Times*, 14 March 1997, pp. B1, 25.

22. S. Mintz and S. Kellogg, *Domestic Revolutions: A Social History of American Family Life*. New York: Free Press, 1988.

23. Arlie R. Hochschild, *The Time Bind: When Work Becomes Home and Home Becomes Work*. New York: Metropolitan Books/Henry Holt, 1997.

24. Sandra Scarr, *Mother Care, Other Care*. New York: Warner Books, 1984.

25. Ellen Galinsky, The Impact of Child Care on Parents. In *Child Care in the 90's*, ed. Alan Booth, pp. 159–171. Hillsdale, NJ: Lawrence Erlbaum, 1992.

26. Holly Tingey, Gary Kiger, and Pamela Riley, Juggling Multiple Roles: Perceptions of Working Mothers. *Social Science Journal* 33(2):183–191, 1996.

27. Shari Thurer, *Myths of Motherhood*. op. cit.

28. Susan Chira, Images of the Perfect Mother: Put Them Together in a Multitude of Ways. *The New York Times*, 8 May 1994, p. 26.

29. Thurer, *Myths of Motherhood*, op. cit.

30. Ethel Spector Person, Working Mothers: Impact on the Self, the Couple, and the Children. In *The Psychology of Today's Woman: New Psychoanalytic Visions*, ed. Toni Bernay and Dorothy Cantor, pp. 121–138. Cambridge, MA: Harvard University Press, 1986.

31. Susan Chira, *A Mother's Place*, op. cit.

32. Barnett and Rivers, *She Works, He Works*. San Francisco: Harper, 1996.

33. Hillary Rodham Clinton, *It Takes a Village and Other Lessons Children Teach Us*. New York: Simon & Schuster, 1996.

34. J. M. Ross, *What Men Want. Mothers, Fathers and Manhood*. Cambridge, MA: Harvard University Press, 1994.

35. James A. Levine, *Working Fathers: New Strategies for Balancing Work and Family*. New York: Addison Wesley, 1997.

36. E. Galinsky and J. T. Bond, Work and Family: The Experiences of Mothers and Fathers in the U.S. Labor Force. In *The American Woman 1996–1997*, ed. Cynthia Costello and Barbara K. Krimgold, p. 96. New York: W. W. Norton, 1996.

37. M. E. Lamb, *The Role of the Father in Child Development*. New York: John Wiley, 1997.

38. Kyle Pruett, *The Nurturing Father*. New York: Warner, 1987.

CHAPTER 3

1. John D. Friesen, *Structural-Strategic Marriage and Family Therapy*. New York: Gardner, 1985.

2. Schiff, The Runaway Mother. *New Yorker*, 10 November 1997, pp. 78–83.

3. Joan Friedman, personal communication, 2 February 1998.

4. Donald W. Winnicott, The Development of the Capacity for Concern. In *The Maturational Processes and the Facilitating Environment*, pp. 73–82. Madison, CT: International Universities Press, 1963.

5. T. Berry Brazelton, *Toddlers and Parents: A Declaration of Independence*. New York: Delta/Seymour Lawrence, 1974.

6. T. Berry Brazelton and Bertrand G. Cramer, *The Earliest Relationship*. New York: Addison Wesley, 1990.

7. Sigmund Freud, Instincts and Their Vicissitudes. *Standard Edition* 14:117–140, 1915.

8. Brazelton, *Toddlers and Parents*, op. cit.

9. T. Berry Brazelton, *On Becoming a Family*. New York: Delacorte, 1981.

10. Penelope Leach, *The Child Care Encyclopedia. A Parents' Guide to the Physical and Emotional Well Being of Children from Birth to Adolescence*. New York: Knopf, 1984.

11. Penelope Leach, *Children First: What Our Society Must Do—and Is Not Doing—for Our Children*. New York: Knopf, 1984.

12. Selma H. Fraiberg, *The Magic Years*. New York: Scribner's, 1959.

13. David Elkind, *A Sympathetic Understanding of the Child: Birth to Sixteen*. New York: Allyn & Bacon, 1974.

14. Jerome Kagan, *The Nature of the Child*. New York: Basic Books, 1984.

15. Lawrence Balter, *Dr. Balter's Child Sense: Understanding and Handling the Common Problems of Infancy and Early Childhood*. New York: Poseidon, 1985.

16. Benjamin Spock, *A Better World for our Children: Rebuilding American Family Values*. Chicago: Contemporary Books, 1996.

17. Benjamin Spock, *Baby and Child Care*. New York: Pocket Books, 1957.

18. Robyn Lynn Leavitt, *Power and Emotion in Infant-Toddler Day Care*. New York: SUNY Press, 1994.

19. Mary D. S. Ainsworth, The Development of Infant–Mother Attachment. In *Review of Child Development Research, vol. 3; Child Development and Social Policy*, ed. B. Caldwell and M. Ricciuti, pp. 1–94. Chicago: University of Chicago Press, 1973.

20. Faye E. Dudden, *Serving Women: Household Service*. Middletown, CT: Wesleyan University Press, 1983.

21. Jonathan Gathhorne-Hardy, *The Unnatural History of the Nanny*. New York: Dial, 1972.

22. Jamaica Kincaid, *Lucy*. New York: Plume/Penguin, 1991.

23. Sigmund Freud, Letter No. 70. *Standard Edition* 1:261–262, 1897.

24. Sigmund Freud, The Interpretation of Dreams. *Standard Edition* 4:247–248, 1900.

25. Sigmund Freud, The Psychopathology of Everyday Life. *Standard Edition* 6:51, 1901.

26. Sigmund Freud, Beyond the Pleasure Principle. *Standard Edition* 18:3–66, 1920.

27. W. W. Meissner, The Earliest Internalizations. In *Self and Object Constancy: Clinical and Theoretical Perspectives*, ed. Ruth F. Lax, Sheldon Bach, and J. Alexis Burland, pp. 29–72. New York: Guilford, 1986.

28. Donald W. Winnicott, *The Maturational Processes and the Facilitating Environment*. Madison, CT: International Universities Press, 1965.

29. John Bowlby, The Nature of the Child's Tie to His Mother. *International Journal of Psycho-Analysis* 39:350–373, 1958.

30. R. A. Spitz, Hospitalism: An Inquiry Into the Genesis of Psychiatric Conditions in Early Childhood. *The Psychoanalytic Study of the Child*. New York: International Universities Press, pp. 53–74, 1954.

31. Mary D. S. Ainsworth, Attachment, Exploration, and Separation Illustrated by the Behavior of One-Year-Olds in a Strange Situation. *Child Development* 41:49–67, 1970.

32. Susan Chira, *A Mother's Place*. New York: Harper Collins, 1998.

33. Leavitt, *Power and Emotion*, op. cit.

34. K. A. Clarke-Stewart, Infant Day Care: Maligned or Malignant? *American Psychologist* 44:266–273, 1989.

35. M. Sheerer and D. Cassidy, An Exploratory Study of Day Care Children and Reunion Time in an Adapted Version of the Strange Situation Experiment. *Child and Youth Care Forum* 22(6):427–439, 1993.

36. Carolee Howes et al., Attachment and Child Care: Relationships with Mother and Caregiver. In *Infant Day Care: The Current Debate*, ed. Nathan Fox and Greta G. Fein, pp. 169–182. Norwood, NJ: Ablex, 1990.

37. Rudolph H. Schaffer and Peggy Emerson, The Development of Social Attachments in Infancy. *Monographs of the Society for Research in Child Development*, No. 94, 1964.

38. Leavitt, *Power and Emotion*, citing M. Lewis, Social Development in Infancy and Early Childhood. In *Handbook of Infant Development*, 2nd ed., ed. J. Osofsky, pp. 419–493. New York: John Wiley, 1987.

39. Jerome Kagan, Family Experience and the Child's Development. *American Psychologist* 34:886–891, 1979.

40. Patricia Nachman, The Maternal Representation. A Comparison of Caregiver- and Mother-Reared Toddlers. *Psychoanalytic Study of the Child* 46:69–90. New Haven, CT: Yale University Press, 1991.

41. Susan Kontos et al., *Quality in Family Child Care*. New York: Teachers' College Press, 1995.

42. C. Howes and P. Stewart, Child's Play with Adults, Toys and Peers: An Examination of Family and Child Influences. *Developmental Psychology* 23:423–430, 1987.

43. Kontos, *Quality in Family Child Care*, op. cit.

44. R. A. Spitz, *The First Year of Life: A Psychoanalytic Study of Normal and Deviant Development of Object Relations*. New York: International Universities Press, 1965.

45. Margaret S. Mahler, Fred Pine, and Anni Bergman, *The Psychological Birth of the Human Infant: Symbiosis and Individuation*. New York: Basic Books, 1975.

46. Laura H. Tessman, *Helping Children Cope with Parting Parents*. Northvale, NJ: Jason Aronson, 1998.

CHAPTER 4

1. William Safire, The Governess: What to Call the Person Who Looks After Your Kids—from Baby Sitter to Mary Poppins. *New York Times Magazine*, 30 November 1997, p. 38.

2. Jonathan Gathhorne-Hardy, *The Unnatural History of the Nanny*. New York: Dial, 1972.

3. Antoine Prost and Gerard Vincent, eds., *A History of Private Life: Riddles of Identity in Modern Times*. Cambridge, MA: Belknap Press of Harvard University Press, 1991.

4. Gathhorne-Hardy, *The Unnatural History of the Nanny*, op. cit.

5. Geraldine Youcha, *Minding the Children*. New York: Scribner's, 1995.

6. *Webster's Seventh New Collegiate Dictionary*. Springfield, MA: G. & C. Merriam, 1970.

7. Patricia Nachman, The Maternal Representation. *Psychoanalytic Study of the Child* 46:69–90. New Haven, CT: Yale University Press, 1991.

8. D. W. Krueger, ed., *The Last Taboo: Money as Symbol and Reality in Psychotherapy and Psychoanalysis*. New York: Guilford, 1986.

9. E. Bergler, *Money and Emotional Conflicts*. New York: International Universities Press, 1985.

CHAPTER 5

1. Jamaica Kincaid, *Lucy*. New York: Plume/Penguin, 1991.

2. Sigmund Freud, The Dynamics of Transference. *Standard Edition* 12:99–108, 1912.

3. Otto Kernberg, An Ego Psychology-Object Relations Theory Approach to the Transference. *Psychoanalytic Quarterly* 56:197–221, 1986.

4. Otto Kernberg, *Love Relations: Normality and Pathology*. New Haven, CT: Yale University Press, 1995.

5. Merton Gill, *The Analysis of Transference*. New York: International Universities Press, 1982.

CHAPTER 6

1. Julia Wrigley, *Other People's Children*. New York: Basic Books, 1995.

2. J. S. Sale, K. Kollenberg, and E. Melinkoff, *The Working Parents' Handbook*. New York: Fireside, 1996.

3. Sandra Scarr, *Mother Care, Other Care*. New York: Warner, 1984.

4. Jean Kassler, The Great Nanny Hunt. *New York Magazine*, 19 July 1993, pp. 34–42.

5. Angela Scalpello, In-Home Child Care: Making the Match. *Working Mother*, April 1997, pp. 24–27.

6. Elaine S. Pelletier, *How to Hire a Nanny: A Complete Step by Step Guide for Parents*. Denver, CO: Andre & Lanier, 1994.

7. D. Helen Susik, *Hiring Home Caregivers: The Family Guide to In-Home Eldercare*. San Luis Obispo, CA: Impact, 1995.

8. Gavin DeBecker, *The Gift of Fear: Survival Signals That Protect Us from Violence*. New York: Little, Brown, 1997.

9. Marc Angel, *The Orphaned Adult*. New York: Insight, 1987.

10. Brian DesRoches, *Your Boss Is Not Your Mother: Creating Autonomy, Respect, and Success at Work*. New York: William Morrow, 1995.

CHAPTER 7

1. Stephen R. Covey, *The Seven Habits of Highly Effective People*. New York: Fireside, 1990.

2. Susan Cheever, The Nanny Track, *New Yorker*, 6 March 1995.

3. Covey, op. cit.

4. Brian DesRoches, *Your Boss Is Not Your Mother*, 1995.

5. Lois Gold, *Between Love and Hate: A Guide to Civilized Divorce*. New York: Plume/Penguin, 1996.

6. D. Helen Susik, *Hiring Caregivers: The Family Guide to In-Home Eldercare*. San Luis Obispo, CA: Impact, 1995.

7. Covey, op. cit.

8. John B. McDevitt and Margaret S. Mahler, Object Constancy, Individuality, and Internalization. In *Self and Object Constancy*. ed. Ruth F. Lax, Sheldon Bach, and J. Alexis Burland, pp. 11–28. New York: Guilford, 1986.

CHAPTER 8

1. Steven P. Shelov and Robert E. Hannemann, eds., *The American Academy of Pediatrics: Caring for Your Baby and Young Child*. New York: Bantam, 1991.

2. National Clearinghouse on Child Abuse and Neglect Information, Washington, DC.

3. Shelov and Hannemann, op. cit.

4. James A. Monteleone, *Recognition of Child Abuse for the Mandated Reporter*. New York: Mosby-Year Book, 1996.

5. Patricia Nachman, The Maternal Representation. *Psychoanalytic Study of the Child* 46:69–90. New Haven, CT: Yale University Press, 1991.

6. Craig Erkus, personal communication, 20 January 1998.

7. Ellen Galinsky and Judy David, *The Preschool Years: Family Strategies That Work—From Experts and Parents*. New York: Ballantine, 1988.

8. Nancy Balaban, When Your Caregiver Says Goodbye. *Working Mother*, March 1997, pp. 38–40.

9. Monteleone, *Recognition of Child Abuse*, op. cit.

10. Claudia Jewett Jarratt, *Helping Children Cope with Separation and Loss*. Boston, MA: Harvard Common Press, 1994.

11. Donald W. Winnicott, Transitional Objects and Transitional Phenomena. In *Through Paediatrics to Psychoanalysis*, pp. 229–242. New York: Basic Books, 1951.

12. Heinz Kohut, *The Analysis of the Self*, New York: International Universities Press, 1971.

CHAPTER 9

1. Tomb Found for Wet Nurse to Future King Tut. AP-Cairo, Egypt. *New York Times*, 8 December 1997.

2. Rosemary Jordano and Marie Oates, Putting the Children First. *New York Times* 9 November 1997, p. 19.

3. Bill Ury and Roger Fisher, *Getting to Yes Without Giving In*. New York: Houghton Mifflin, 1992.

4. Stephen R. Covey, *The Seven Habits of Highly Effective Families*. New York: Golden, 1997.

Index

About the Authors

Joseph A. Cancelmo, Psy.D., is a graduate and member of the Institute for Psychoanalytic Training and Research (IPTAR) in New York City. He serves as Administrator for the IPTAR Membership Society Board, a faculty member of IPTAR's Introductory Psychoanalytic Program, and a supervisor and Coordinator of Outreach for the IPTAR Clinical Center. He is a member of the International Psychoanalytical Society, a certified Psychologist, and a Nationally Certified School Psychologist. Dr. Cancelmo is an adjunct faculty member and clinical supervisor at the New York Counseling and Guidance Service and at Pace University's Center for Psychological Services. He maintains a private practice in New York City in psychoanalysis, psychotherapy, and parent consultation.

Dr. Carol Bandini holds a doctorate in Religious Studies from the University of Strasbourg, France, a Masters of Social Work from New York University, and a Masters in History from Fordham University, New York. She has trained as a psychoanalyst at the Institute of Psychoanalytic Training and Research where she is now a member, serving on the Institute Board of Training and teaching in the Introductory Psychoanalytic Program. Dr. Bandini has been influenced by her experiences and training at the Institute for Bioenergetic Analysis during which she has worked extensively with patients with psychosomatic illness. She is a Training Fellow and has taught abroad at the International Institute for Bioenergetic Analysis. Dr. Bandini maintains a private practice in psychoanalysis and psychotherapy in New York City and in Summit, New Jersey.